SOCIAL WORK AND LAW

SOCIAL WORKERS, THEIR CLIENTS AND THE LAW

AUSTRALIA
The Law Book Company Ltd.
Sydney: Melbourne: Brisbane

CANADA AND U.S.A.
The Carswell Company Ltd.
Agincourt, Ontario

INDIA
N.M. Tripathi Private Ltd.
Bombay
and
Eastern Law House (Private) Ltd.
Calcutta
M.P.P. House
Bangalore

ISRAEL
Steimatzky's Agency Ltd.
Jerusalem: Tel Aviv: Haifa

MALAYSIA : SINGAPORE : BRUNEI
Malayan Law Journal (Pte.) Ltd.
Singapore

NEW ZEALAND
Sweet and Maxwell (N.Z.) Ltd.
Auckland

PAKISTAN
Pakistan Law House
Karachi

SOCIAL WORK AND LAW

SOCIAL WORKERS, THEIR CLIENTS AND THE LAW

Michael Zander
Professor of Law at the London School of Economics

Third Edition

LONDON
SWEET & MAXWELL
1981

First edition 1974
Second edition 1977
Third edition 1981

Published by
Sweet & Maxwell Ltd. of
11 New Fetter Lane, London
and printed in Great Britain by
Thomson Litho Ltd.,
East Kilbride, Scotland

British Library Cataloguing in Publication Data

Zander, Michael
  Social workers, their clients and the law.—
  3rd ed.—(Social work and law).
    1. Law—England
    2. Public welfare—Law and legislation
    —England
    I. Title   II. Series
    344.2'0024362   KD665.S6

  0-421-27930-3

PREFACE

This book grew out of the work of the Study Group on legal studies for social workers set up in 1972 by the Central Council for Education and Training in Social Work. The author was a member of that Study Group. Its Report* concluded that social workers should be taught four kinds of law. The first was "professional law," the law which concerns the carrying out by social workers of their professional duties. So social workers obviously need to be taught such matters as the duties of local authorities in regard to children in care.

In addition to this, however, the Committee thought it essential that social workers have a grasp of three other aspects of law. One it described as "law and society," the general function and nature of law. The second was the "administration of law," the structure and workings of the courts and tribunals and of the legal profession. The third it called "general law," the law that affects the day-to-day life of the client as an ordinary citizen, relating, for example, to his position as a tenant, consumer, recipient of social security or victim of an accident.

It appeared to the Study Group that the number of textbooks on law written specifically with the social work student in mind was limited. This work was therefore originally conceived to fill part of this gap. Its aim is mainly to provide a basic text for social work students (and their teachers) on "law and society," "the administration of law" and especially "general law." It does not include "professional law."

Such highly selective and necessarily brief treatment of legal issues is open to the objection that it will do more harm than good. A little learning can be a dangerous thing. In this area, however, no learning can be even more dangerous. Ideally, of course, every social worker's client with a legal problem should receive advice from a fully qualified lawyer. But as the Study Group's Report itself said "in some situations the hope that the client will go to a lawyer is unrealistic. In practice, the choice is often between getting advice from a social worker or getting no advice at all."

In the amount of time available in the typical two-year course it is not possible to turn social workers into mini-lawyers. But the book is based on the belief, expressed by the Study Group's

*"Legal Studies in Social Work Education", published by the Council in August 1974.

Report, that a useful purpose is nevertheless served by teaching students a basic minimum of knowledge about some of the most common legal problems likely to come their way. Such knowledge, sketchy though it may be, may nevertheless be of the greatest value to their clients—either in enabling the social worker to solve the problem directly, or at least, to recognise the existence of a problem that requires more expert help and to know how to go about getting it.

In addition to being intended for teachers and students in social work courses, it is hoped that the book will also be useful for social workers in the field as a ready reference work to help them help their clients. (Some of the detail of the book is included purely for this reason—students should not be made to learn all this detail by heart.) Too many clients in the past have endured the painful consequences of festering or unsolved legal problems because neither they nor the social worker recognised the problem as a legal one or knew what to do about it. The book is different from most written on the law in that it does not belabour the reader with endless citations of cases, statutes and other supporting authorities. Social workers will only rarely find use for such references and it was thought better not to burden the text with much useless learning.

Unless otherwise indicated the law stated is that at January 1, 1981. The third edition of the book is very similar to the first—brought up to date and slightly expanded. The Chapter on Social Security Benefits has been wholly re-written and the landlord–tenant chapter has required substantial changes especially to take account of the Housing Act 1980 but the temptation to add whole new sections has been resisted, not because the present coverage is complete but because the object of the book remains to present the basic minimum of information.

January 1981   MICHAEL ZANDER

Note: This book does not cover Scottish law.

CONTENTS

vii

TABLE OF CASES

List of Abbreviations

A.C.   Appeal Cases
All E.R.   All England Law Reports
E.G.   Estates Gazette
W.L.R.   Weekly Law Reports

TABLE OF STATUTES

1 The Nature of Law

Law is, first and foremost, a body of rules. But the rules are of a particular character, for they are invested with the special significance attached in any community to the word "law." One aspect of this special meaning is that the rules are felt to be binding. A law that is not binding is a contradiction in terms. In one sense, of course, all rules are binding, but legal rules are widely felt to be more binding than others. One practical consequence is that law tends to be more of a conservative force than other systems of rules - less easily malleable, less responsive to changing needs.

Secondly, the word "law" is associated with the concept of sanction. It is often said that one obeys the law or it is uniquely binding because failure to comply with its dictates may be visited by unpleasant consequences in the shape of the intervention of policemen, courts, prisons and the like. Fear is seen to be an important element in obedience to law.

To some extent this view is based on an unduly narrow view of the scope of law, for it concentrates primarily on the criminal law which is almost all of the "Don't Do That" variety and where penalties are established for those who offend. Most law, in reality, is not of this kind. The crude admonition Don't Do That is much less frequently a form of law than the more sophisticated If You Want to Achieve Your Aim, Do It This Way. If you wish to form a partnership, make a will, marry, adopt a child, agree a contract or transfer property the law provides for the form and procedures that should be adopted. The failure to get your will witnessed as required in law by two witnesses results, not in penalties for the testator, but in an invalid will. The failure to comply with the legal rules regarding adoption simply means that the aim of adopting a child cannot be realised. So failure to comply with the law in very many cases, though it has consequences, does not have penalties in the ordinary sense. The belief that sanctions are crucial to the idea of law must therefore be modified to take account of the fact that there are more positive reasons why people obey law than simple fear. In a great many instances they follow the law because it provides a means for them to secure benefits or advantages they could not attain in any other way.

A third connotation of the word "law" is a system of control to which even the rulers are subject. We speak of a government of laws not of men and this constitutional principle is regarded as fundamental in a democracy. It means that the rulers for the time being must abide by the existing law save in so far as it has been altered by the duly approved procedures for changing the law. Moreover, the concept implies that these duly approved procedures will not be abused to enact law that is morally offensive or corrupt. An evil, totalitarian regime which captures the machinery of the state, can, of course, give a kind of legality to its policies by using the previously accepted modes of law-making. Hitler passed even morally obnoxious measures through the ordinary processes of legislation and thereby secured for them from most members of the community the particular respect attached to the concept "law." But this is the opposite of what one understands to be "the rule of law." When President Nixon in 1973 dismissed the Special Watergate Prosecutor, Professor Archibald Cox, he may, according to the strict letter of the law, have had the power to do so, but his act was in defiance of the rule of law. For the President to sack the person investigating the guilt of the White House was to violate the basic precept that no man shall be a judge in his own cause, which is precisely what is meant by the rule of law. The rule of law therefore connotes the protection of the citizens from abuse of power by the rulers.

Another fundamental feature of law, at least in modern democratic societies, is that it attaches value to the concept of equality. Today, everyone is said to be equal before the law irrespective of race, colour, religion or economic status. The content of the concept of equality is the freedom of all to come before the courts, the independence of the judges to dispose of disputes even-handedly and on their real merits and the pressures that inhibit both Parliament and the courts from making laws which discriminate unfairly between one class of citizen and another.

Needless to say, massive inequalities continue to exist. It is relatively easy to say that all are free to use the courts and even to provide a legal aid system to make it practically possible for a poor man to have a lawyer to represent him. But it is extremely difficult, if not impossible, to eradicate the whole range of advantages enjoyed by the rich over the poor in regard to use of the legal system. Formal equality, in the sense of the freedom to use the courts and to state one's case is one thing; real, substantial equality is quite another. But formal equality, though not to be confused with real equality, is nevertheless of value. Genuine gains are made when legal representation is provided for the poor to enable them to present their cases before the courts. Moreover, the gain is not simply in terms of the adage that justice must be seen to be done. Whilst the presence of an advocate cannot guarantee that justice will be done, it makes it somewhat more likely.

Another meaning attached to the word "law" is that of authority and proper procedures. A rule represents the law only if it has been produced by those persons or agencies in the community vested with the authority to produce law. Thus, if the Lord Chancellor in the course of debate in the House of Lords gives his opinion on a point of law, his speech makes no mark on the corpus of the law. If he makes the same remarks in deciding a case that he has heard in his judicial capacity, his speech is a statement of the law. Moreover, in so far as it differs from previous formulations of the relevant rule, his speech may have changed the law.

In our society, law is made primarily by two agencies - the legislature and the courts. Parliament pours out statutes - in 1979 no less than 60 measures running to 1,431 pages in the statute book were passed into law.

The law-making of the judges is, by comparison, much less extensive. But any decision by a judge on a disputed point of law is to some extent a piece of law-making. Frequently, the extent of the change in the law is small; it amounts to no more than a clarification, elaboration or application of an existing rule. But sometimes the courts engage in a much more sweeping form of law-making - for instance, by inventing a new cause of action or by abolishing some old rule which had previously been thought to be inconvenient or unjust.

The concept of authority and of proper procedures in our system also brings into play the doctrine of precedent, which relies on the hierarchy of courts. At the apex is the House of Lords whose decisions bind all lower courts - though not, since 1966, the House of Lords itself. Below it is the Court of Appeal, which is generally bound by its own decisions, and below that, the High Court whose decisions do not bind later High Court judges.

If a decision in an earlier case is relevant and it emanates from a higher court, the doctrine of precedent requires that it be applied. Of course, everything depends on the initial determination that it *is* relevant, but lawyers have developed standards of reasoning which make this process *somewhat* predictable. It is by no means automatic, nor should it be thought that there is no room for subjective choice by the judge. But when all allowances have been made for the role of the judge's private preference for one rule over a proposed alternative, it remains true that, to a considerable extent, the decision as to relevance is one dictated by processes of reasoning to which most lawyers would subscribe.

The doctrine of precedent can seem in one sense to be a substitute for thought. The judge follows an earlier decision simply because the rule was laid down by a higher court in an earlier case. This is one of the ways in which the natural conservatism of the law is expressed. On the other hand, to follow precedent is to create stability and thereby, not only to increase public confidence in the law, but also in practical ways, to make it easier for lawyers to advise their clients. If the law were constantly in a state of flux, no one could ever arrange his affairs in reliance on it - and the creation of the feeling of reliance is one of the crucial functions of any legal system.

It is important, therefore, that the right balance be found between the urge towards stability and predictability, on the one hand, and the need for flexibility and a capacity for change on the other. In our system, Parliament is absolutely free to change the law. No Parliament can bind a later Parliament. Even so solemn a commitment as entry into the Common Market can, so far as English law is concerned, be undone by some future Parliament. But the courts are compelled to a considerable extent to follow precedents. Moreover, they often feel obliged to follow precedents even when they are not technically binding. So the Court of Appeal or the House of Lords may follow a precedent of which they disapprove because it is well established and its removal would upset people's reasonable calculations or because to uproot it requires a judgment as to social or economic values which may be felt more appropriate for the legislature to make. Quite often a court will say that a rule which it is technically free to change should be changed, if at all, only by Parliament.

There can be no doubt that law reform through Parliament has many advantages over law reform by the courts. For one thing the parliamentary process is more open to pressure from those interested in the particular issue. Those concerned can make their views known - through the press, through lobbying and through the ordinary processes of public debate. None of these operate on the judges. Secondly, those who promote legislation can consult a much wider range of expert opinion than is possible for the courts. The judges must rely for their view of what the law is, or ought to be, on argument presented by counsel for the two parties. A Minister interested in introducing legislation can consult as widely as he wishes. The groundwork on law reform subjects will often be done by the Law Commission, whose function is to keep the entire body of the law under review and to make suggestions for its improvement. Obviously, the Law Commission or the Minister can do a more thorough job of preparing the law reform proposals than is possible for the courts.

Moreover, the legislative solution can be more complete. A judicial decision can only lay down a rule of law for the situations covered by similar sets of facts. Finally, law reform by the courts is contrary to the basic democratic principle that law-making should mainly be in the hands of the elected rather than of the appointed representatives of the people.

But in spite of all these considerations, there can be no doubt that the judges retain, and will always retain, an important role as law reformers. If they were to leave the solution of all problems to the legislature, many would never get solved or only after years of delay. If the courts were to refuse to turn their hand to keeping the law abreast of changing times, there would be an outcry against the rigidity and inflexibility of the legal system. Most judges may tend to be conservative in inclination but even the least bold may, in some circumstances, have no hesitation in rooting out a precedent which he believes to be obstructive of justice. Certainly, the history of the common law over the past hundreds of years shows many examples of judges improving the law by reshaping it, by pruning dead branches or by developing new solutions.

The actual scope and reach of the law is, of course, always in a state of change as both Parliament and the courts make and unmake laws. In one era, for instance, the community treats as crimes conduct that in another age is regarded as not properly the subject of the intervention of the law. Homosexual acts between consenting adults, suicide and abortion are areas in which the law has in recent years retreated. By contrast, sex discrimination and racial discrimination are areas in which the law has recently been expanded.

Whether law ought or not to be used to regulate conduct in any particular field of human relations is more of a social— political than a legal question. Is the social problem sufficiently serious to require a law? If yes, can a law improve things? Should it make the conduct in question a crime? Will the law be enforceable and if so, at what cost in terms of enforcement agencies and other repercussions? These are the questions that inevitably pose themselves whenever a present law is considered for abolition or a new rule is considered for enactment.

The fact that something is governed by law does not of course mean that the problem will be cured. Certain types of conduct are not easily amenable to regulation by law. Prohibition in the United States was a classic instance of a well-intentioned law failing utterly to achieve its purpose. Worse, it led to the wholesale flouting of the law even by ordinarily law-abiding citizens and thereby weakened the general respect for the law. At the same time it also produced a massive increase in organised crime. A vexed problem of a somewhat similar kind in recent British history is the question to what extent law ought to regulate the relations between management and labour, or should control wages and prices. The implacable opposition of the unions both to the 1971 Industrial Relations Act and to the Heath Government's statutory Prices and Incomes policy raised the question as to whether a government can, in practice, legislate in the face of the active non-cooperation of a powerful minority of the country. The painful lesson of these events may be that opposition by those who have the strength seriously to harm the country's economic situation through strikes and other economic pressure can prevent even a strong government from governing. Whether this was the fault of the goverment in unwisely passing highly controversial legislation or of the union movement in unreasonably resisting laws passed by a democractically elected government, is a matter of opinion. What cannot seriously be doubted is that when the law is subjected to such severe tension, there is a real danger that it will lose some of its force.

The authority of the word "law" will therefore depend on the skill and wisdom of the rulers in using it appropriately. At least in a democracy a determined minority prepared to take strong action against a law it dislikes can cause a vast amount of damage to the rule of law. To avoid this and yet continue to govern on controversial issues is one of the highest political arts.

Fortunately, however, these crises of authority are rare. Most of the law does not arouse such acute tensions in society. For the most part, the law is unquestioned and can, more or less effectively, do its job of regulating and facilitating human activities.

Law is, however, not always synonymous with justice. Until uprooted or modified, a rule of law remains valid even if it is demonstrably unjust. Naturally the law and the legal system aspire to achieve justice but frequently they fail to realise this objective. Often, for instance, the law lags behind contemporary values and becomes unjust through being outmoded. Or rules are followed slavishly without sufficient regard to the question whether they could not be adapted or even abolished. Lawyers tend to fear that if unjust laws could be avoided simply because they were unjust, the stability of the law would be at the mercy of sentiment and emotion. It is after all much easier to obtain agreement as to what a rule of law is, than as to whether and to what extent it is unjust and, if so, what ought to replace it.

The problem is aggravated by the fact that many judges sincerely believe that by applying an unjust rule they may actually be serving a higher form of justice, than if they were to twist, avoid or alter the law to meet the needs of the case. This approach is in fact very common amongst English judges. When a point of law is argued in an English courtroom, most of the argument is devoted to the question of what the law *is*, little to what it *ought to be*. The rule that emerges from this process is then applied whether or not it happens to give a just result in the particular circumstances.

The concept of justice evoked by this approach is perhaps somewhat abstract. Some judges, however, of whom Lord Denning is probably the best known, approach justice more directly. Where most of his brethren start with the search for the law, Lord Denning begins with the search for justice - in the layman's sense. For him the main question is whether he can find a way to achieve what he conceives to be the just result. Providing a judge does not misuse the technical rules of the law, providing he respects the proper methodology of lawyer-like decision-making, such an approach would seem not merely legitimate but desirable.

2 Dealing with a Legal Problem

1. *WHETHER TO USE A LAWYER*

Clients and social workers alike frequently fail to recognise legal problems when they see them. There is no way around this other than to widen one's knowledge of the situations in which the solution to a problem is affected by the law. Most people in the community seem to realise that buying a house is a legal problem, possibly because it is thought to be virtually impossible to purchase a house without going to a lawyer.

But there appear to be large areas of legal problems which are like virgin land, unknown and mysterious to the ordinary citizen. He rarely thinks of going to seek legal advice when the landlord fails to do the repairs or gives him a notice to quit, when his social security payments are less than he thinks he should get, if he pays too much rent, buys defective goods or is sued for debt. In all of these situations the potential value of seeking advice from a professional is not understood.

As a result people frequently suffer real losses. They leave premises unaware of the fact that they are protected by the Rent Acts, they accept ludicrously inadequate offers of settlement from the insurance company in the belief that they are being fairly treated, they continue to pay extortionate rents unaware of the right to ask for a reduction from the rent officer.

There are, of course, many reason why potential clients do not go to lawyers. One important one is undoubtedly fear of the cost and ignorance of the scope and content of the legal aid system. Another is the shortage or even non-existence of lawyers in the particular neighbourhood and a reluctance to travel into other areas to seek advice. A third is the feeling that some people have that lawyers are not for the likes of them — either because they perceive lawyers as stuffy, middle class, formal and stilted or because they think of them as representing primarily "the other side" (landlords, creditors, the police, the insurance company, etc.). Also the middle-class member of the community is, on the whole, more likely than others to think of the legal system as being there at least partly to protect him and as being therefore available to correct wrongs done to him. The less advantaged person, including many who are by no means poor, may tend to see the law as more of a hostile or threatening force which generally acts upon him rather than responding to his needs. The idea that the legal system can be made responsive to the demands of the ordinary person and that it can provide benefits in cash or kind, as well as pains and penalties, is not one that is widely understood.

Not that all legal problems should necessarily be taken to lawyers. For one thing, there could never be sufficient lawyers to make such an aim a practical reality. But quite apart from the shortage of lawyers, there will be many situations in which the services of a trained professional would be unnecessary and where advice from some less legally qualified person might be perfectly adequate. The more the para-professional or semi-qualified person is fitted to advise, the more widely the legal system can be made effectively available to the community.

If the problem is one that concerns employment or injuries suffered during work, a trade union adviser may be available. (Some unions are expanding their legal advisory services into wider fields.) If the issue is one involving the position of the tenants, there may be a tenants' association that could help. On consumer problems there may be a local consumers' advice centre. On social security and supplementary benefits the local branch of the Child Poverty Action Group or a claimants' union are expert advisers better qualified to assist than most lawyers. If the problem is drugs-related, an organisation such as Release, is perhaps the most likely source for knowledgeable help. Moreover, in addition to the considerable range of such specialist lay or para-professional advisers, there are also generalist organisations of which the Citizens' Advice Bureau is by far the most important. CABs exist throughout the country and provide free advice on a vast range of problems, many of which are legal. They also tend to have reasonably well-developed links with, and knowledge about, the local lawyers and can be used as a source of advice by social workers as to which lawyers should be consulted for particular types of problems.

It is also worth noting that the courts have now fully accepted that the lay litigant is entitled to bring someone to help him with the complexities of the legal proceedings. In *McKenzie* v. *McKenzie* [1970] P. 33, the Court of Appeal permitted a party in a divorce case to be aided by an Australian barrister who sat by him to prompt and make suggestions on the handling of the case. This ruling has resulted in a new concept - the "McKenzie man," someone, whether legally qualified or not, who assists the layman in his court case. In the view of most judges the concept does not however extend to actual advocacy. Social workers who go into court with a client to help him can rely on the *McKenzie* ruling to justify their role. If the McKenzie man is a professional person (solicitor, or otherwise), the courts will often allow his fees if the lay litigant succeeds in his case.

One difficult question for the social worker adviser, however, is *when* to send a client to a lawyer or other more legally qualified person. Obviously, if the legal component of the situation passes unrecognised, this question will never arise. But if the social worker appreciates that the problem is legal or at least partly legal, the question will often occur of whether the client should be advised to take the problem to a lawyer.

It is impossible to be dogmatic about this. Much will depend on the particular problem, on the level of expertise of the social worker, on the practical availability of competent professional legal advisers and on some realistic assessment of the seriousness of the situation and the possible benefits of help from a professional. In general, if there are local lawyers who practise in that field it would probably be wise to err on the side of caution and to send a client on more, rather than less, frequently. At the least, a social worker should always know a lawyer or two in the area who can be approached informally over the telephone to discuss briefly whether the problem warrants referral to a solicitor.

2. *WHERE TO LOOK UP THE LAW*

The best general compilation on law that ought to be available to social workers is the *Citizens' Advice Notes (CANS)*, a loose-leaf service on a great variety of legal problems. It is published by the National Council of Social Service, 26 Bedford Square, London WC1B 3 HU, Tel: 01-636 4066, price £21 initially and then £14.50 per year to keep it up to date.

Another publication that should be available is the *LAG Bulletin* published by the Legal Action Group. This is Britains's only poverty law journal. It appears monthly and deals in a highly practical way with the legal problems that face the poor. It costs £18.00 for individuals, libraries or voluntary organisations or £28.00 for solicitors' firms, or local authorities and is available from LAG, 28A Highgate Road, London NW5 1NS, Tel: 01-485 1189. Every local authority social work department should be a subscriber.

Apart from this, there are of course innumerable books on the different aspects of the law treated in this work.

3. *THE LEGAL PROFESSION*

One of the most important things to be learnt by any person who is in frequent touch with citizens with legal problems is how to direct them to lawyers. It is obviously vital, in particular, that one knows who is entitled to free or subsidised legal services under the state's legal aid scheme.

Lay clients with problems that need the help of lawyers must take them to solicitors. The solicitors' branch of the legal profession has the monopoly of the right of direct access to the client. Barristers are only brought into a problem on the instructions of a solicitor. They number only 4,000 or so and work primarily in London and the main provincial cities. Most barristers do mainly advocacy.

Solicitors number some 30,000 in private practice and are spread throughout the country. In addition, there is a growing (but still very small) number of lawyers employed on salaries paid out of public funds to work in the 30 or so law centres. These are run variously by local authorities, the Urban Aid programme and the Lord Chancellor's Office. From the point of view of social workers, this movement is of special potential value since the lawyers working in such centres are likely to be particularly concerned with, and knowledgeable about, the kinds of problem affecting the most deprived. Also, normally law centres provide services that are altogether free, whereas the legal aid scheme is subject to a possible contribution from the client.

The organisation which runs the solicitors' profession is the Law Society, 113 Chancery Lane, London WC2A 1LP, Tel: 01-242 1222. There are also Local Law Socities in each area. The organisation which concerns itself with the promotion of legal services for the disadvantaged is the Legal Action Group (LAG), mentioned above. The organisation which represents law centres is the Law Centres Federation, 164 North Gower Street, London NW1, Tel: 01-387 8570.

4. *HOW TO REFER A CLIENT*

It is obviously desirable that social workers who refer clients to lawyers have some idea of which lawyers to recommend. To aid this process, the Law Society has in recent years published legal aid Referral Lists (also known as Solicitors Lists) for the different parts of the country showing the firms and legal advice centres in each area and the work they do. The lists are distributed free of charge to all sorts of lay referral agencies. Social work departments should be able to get one from the Local Law Society or the Law Society in London, or through the nearest Citizens' Advice Bureau. It will however be important for those using such lists to supplement them with their own - especially since the official lists only give details of firms and not of individuals within the firms. (The Law Society is however experimenting with a new system of including the specialties of individual solicitors within firms.)

The client should, naturally, be allowed to choose any name on the list, but in the (common) event that he has no basis for making a selection and desires help, it *is* permissible for the social worker to guide his choice by indicating the firms that may be of special assistance to him. In the past, lay referral agencies have felt diffident about directing clients to individual firms - fearing that this would, in some way, be unprofessional practice. More recently, however, it has come to be recognised that clients need guidance and that it is not improper for the referral agency to attempt to help the client find the lawyers best suited to his problem. In 1973 for instance Citizens' Advice Bureaux were advised by their National Association that "every bureau should provide specific help to enquirers in choosing a suitable solicitor.

Normally an enquirer should be given a choice, but a choice
of solicitors all of whom are felt will deal competently with
the enquirer's problem.''

The Law Society has no rule which makes this irregular,
other than the rule which prevents solicitors from unfairly
attracting business to themselves. It would therefore be
wrong for a lay referral agency, such as a social-work department, to come to some form of arrangement (whether
explicit or implicit) to send all the available business to one
out of the several competing firms in the area. The Law
Society would be likely to act on a complaint from one of
the excluded firms and could bring disciplinary proceedings
against the favoured solicitors. (No action could be taken
against the lay referral person or agency, since the Law
Society has no jurisdiction over them.)

But there would be no objection if the lay agency simply
decided for itself, on the basis of its experience, that clients
of one kind ought to be sent to firms A, B or C, whilst clients
with another type of problem should normally be sent to
firms C, D or E. A client presenting the first type of problem
would then be shown the list and told that firms A, B and C
were the ones likely to be most helpful.

Where possible, clients should be given a choice of at least
two firms, but in some areas this may, in practice, not be
feasible. There may only be one firm within a reasonable
distance or only one firm that the lay agency considers suitable for the particular kind of problem in issue. In these circumstances it would be quite legitimate for the client to be
told that this was the situation.

When referring a client to a solicitor, it is always desirable
to telephone the firm to make an actual appointment.
Experience shows that simply to leave the client to make his
own approach often results in none being made. Sometimes,
the social worker may even feel it necessary to accompany
the client to the appointment — partly to ensure that the
client in fact goes and, partly to act as interpreter between an
inarticulate client and a lawyer whose advice may need to be
explained in simple terms by someone familiar with the
client's particular personality and situation.

5. *THE STATE LEGAL AID SCHEME FOR PROVIDING LEGAL SERVICES TO THE INDIGENT*

A client whose means qualify him for the legal aid scheme can obtain help from lawyers either without any charge or for a reduced cost. The help can take one of two forms — first, out-of-court advice or assistance; secondly, aid with actual court proceedings.

(a) *Advice and Assistance (the "Green Form Scheme")*

A client with a legal problem who qualifies under the means test is entitled to go to any solicitor participating in the scheme (most do), to ask for oral or written advice or assistance. It is then entirely within the discretion of the solicitor what work he undertakes within the State scheme. He may write letters, negotiate, vet or draft a document (including a will or a conveyance) and even prepare an argument for the client to present in a court or tribunal. The only limitation is that the lawyer must not go beyond £40* worth of work (£55 in divorce cases) without getting the permission of the local legal aid office. With permission, however, the lawyer can do as much work under the scheme as the case requires - short of advocacy, for which a separate application must normally be made. (But since 1980 in matrimonial proceedings in magistrates' courts the green form scheme can be used also for advocacy and the Lord Chancellor can extend this to other proceedings.)

The scheme came into effect in April 1973. It replaced the old Legal Advice and Claims Certificate schemes. Upon its introduction the Law Society also announced the abolition of the Voluntary Legal Advice scheme under which anyone, without regard to means, could get half an hour's advice on payment of £1. However, subsequently the Law Society agreed to introduce a voluntary scheme whereby a client, irrespective of means, is charged a flat rate sum of £5 per half hour. Most firms operate this Fixed Fee Scheme for diagnostic interviews.

---

*Formerly £25.

The means test†

To qualify for the new scheme the applicant must qualify on both income and capital (or savings).

Income. Income must not be more than £85 take-home pay, *i.e.* after deduction of national insurance contributions and income tax. For those with family commitments the £85 figure is increased:

for husband or wife add	£24.45
for each child under 11 add	£10.95
for each child of 11 but under 16 add	£16.35
for each child of 16 but under 18 add	£19.65
for each dependant over 18 add	£25.60

Capital. Capital must not be over £600 for a single person with no dependants:

> for one dependant the figure is £200
> for two dependants the figure is £320
> for three dependents the figure is £380
> for each subsequent dependant add £60

To calculate capital take the value of all savings and assets but do not count:
The value of household furniture and effects, personal clothing, tools or implements of trade or the value of any house owned by the applicant.

Anyone in receipt of supplementary benefit or family income supplement is automatically eligible for the scheme unless his savings are outside the capital limits.

Capital and earnings of husband and wife have to be added unless they are separated or unless the problem is one in which they have opposing interests.

† The legal aid means-test limits change from time to time. The latest figures should always be obtainable from the local legal aid offices, the local Citizens' Advice Bureau or the Law Society. The figures given here are as at January 1981.

Client's contribution

If the applicant has take-home pay ("disposable income") of between £40 and £85, he will have to pay a contribution on a sliding scale.

If disposable income			is not more than £40 a week the contribution is £Nil
,,	,,	,, exceeds £40 but not	£50 a week £ 5
,,	,,	,, ,, £50 ,,	£53 ,, £ 9
,,	,,	,, ,, £53 ,,	£56 ,, £13
,,	,,	,, ,, £56 ,,	£59 ,, £17
,,	,,	,, ,, £59 ,,	£62 ,, £21
,,	,,	,, ,, £62 ,,	£65 ,, £25
,,	,,	,, ,, £65 ,,	£68 ,, £29
,,	,,	,, ,, £68 ,,	£71 ,, £33
,,	,,	,, ,, £71 ,,	£74 ,, £37
,,	,,	,, ,, £74 ,,	£77 ,, £41
,,	,,	,, ,, £77 ,,	£80 ,, £45
,,	,,	,, ,, £80 ,,	£85 ,, £49

The solicitor is not obliged to ask for the contribution, but if he does not do so he is out of pocket to that extent. He can, however, agree to its being paid in instalments.

The charge

If the solicitor succeeds in recovering money for the client, that money is applied in the first instance to reimburse the fund for any of the costs, over and above the client's contribution. So, if the client's contribution was £10 and the total legal costs involved in recovering £100 was £40 the fund will demand the first £30 (the difference between the client's contribution and the actual costs). The client will therefore receive only £70, plus whatever proportion of his costs has been recovered from the other party. It is this charge which explains why the legal advice and assistance scheme can rarely be used for small claims — since the client who pays a contribution in such cases will rarely see any profit from the transaction.

(b) *Legal Aid for Court Proceedings*

If the problem is one which appears to involve proceedings that will go to court, the proper course is to apply for ordinary traditional legal aid. This now applies to all courts but not to tribunals[1] (other than the Lands Tribunal and the Employment Appeal Tribunal). Legal aid for a court case provides the assistance of a solicitor and, if necessary, of a barrister.

Two tests have to be satisfied — a merits test and a means test.

The merits test

For civil proceedings the test is whether a competent solicitor would advise a reasonable client who had the means to spend his own money in bringing (or, as the case may be, defending), the proceedings. In criminal cases the test is whether it is in the interests of justice that legal aid be granted. It is almost always considered to be in the interests of justice for legal aid to be granted if the trial is to be at the Crown Court — whether the defendant intends to plead guilty or not guilty. In the case of trials before magistrates, legal aid should be granted if the defendant faces loss of liberty or livelihood or serious damage to his reputation. He should also get legal aid if, for any reason, he cannot be expected to do himself justice without a lawyer — because the case raises a question of law, or because he has personal characteristics which make it unlikely that he can conduct his case sufficiently well on his own.

To qualify for the civil scheme the applicant must be within the limits for both income and capital. The limits are, however, not precisely those set out for the advice and assistance scheme.[2]

Income. Disposable income must not exceed £4,075 plus allowance for dependants. If it is between £1,700 and £4,075 the client will be asked to pay a contribution.

To calculate disposable income, take actual weekly income and add Child Benefits and any other weekly income such as Family Income Supplement, plus any weekly income of the applicant's husband or wife (unless they are not living together or unless the case involves a contest between them). Deduct: income tax and national insurance contributions

---

[1] The Royal Commission on Legal Services recommended in 1979 that legal aid be extended to tribunals.
[2] The figures given are those at January 1981.

paid by the household; reasonable expenses incurred in travelling to and from work; weekly mortgage payments or rent and rates; the appropriate amount for dependants (the same amounts as under the legal advice and assistance scheme see p. 16 above); plus the first £200 of income derived from capital. Deduct also any weekly payments made to a husband or wife living apart from the applicant, any weekly maintenance for a former husband or wife or for a child, relative, or dependant not living with the applicant. There is also a discretion to make an allowance for long hire purchase commitments for essentials. The sum arrived at is net weekly disposable income and must be multiplied by 52 to give an annual figure.

Capital. Disposable capital must normally not be more than £2,500. If it is between £1,200 and £2,500, the applicant will be asked to pay a contribution.

To calculate disposable capital, take the actual aggregate value of savings, shares, bank accounts, sums which could be borrowed on insurance policies and the fair market value of realisable assets such as car, jewellery, etc., but ignore the value of the home, of household furniture, clothing, tools and implements of trade.

Assessment of contribution in civil cases

If the applicant has disposable income below £1,700 *and* disposable capital of under £1,200 he pays no contribution.

If the applicant has disposable income of under £1,700 but disposable capital of between £1,200 and £2,500 he pays a contribution out of capital alone.

If the applicant has disposable income of between £1,700 and £4,075 but disposable capital of under £1,200 he pays a contribution out of income alone.

If the applicant has disposable income of between £1,700 and £4,075 and disposable capital of between £1,200 and £2,500 he pays a contribution out of both income and capital.

If the applicant has disposable income of over £4,075 *or* disposable capital of over £2,500 he is not entitled to legal aid at all.

Income. To assess the contribution, take actual disposable income and deduct from it the ceiling for free legal aid, now

£1,700. One-quarter of the resulting sum is the amount of contribution from income. So, if the disposable income is £2,700, the contribution from income is one-quarter of £1,000 or £250.

Capital. To assess the contribution from capital take any excess of disposable capital over the ceiling for free legal aid, now £1,200. The whole of such sum is the contribution.

The actual assessment of means for legal aid purposes in civil cases is undertaken by the Supplementary Benefits authorities. In criminal cases, it is done normally by the courts' officers themselves.

Payment of contribution

In civil cases, the applicant is invariably asked to start making payments towards his contributions as soon as he agrees to an offer of legal aid. Normally he will be asked to make his payments in twelve monthly instalments. If, at the end of the case, the contributions come to more than the actual costs of the case he is entitled to a refund of any balance.

In criminal cases, a contribution in advance is occasionally asked for but it is almost always of a very small sum, usually £5 or £10. Contributions are fixed after the case has ended, in the light of the defendant's capacity to pay, which commonly varies according to whether he has been given a prison sentence. The longer the sentence, the less likely that any contribution will be ordered. Usually none is ordered.

The means test in criminal cases

In criminal cases, the means test is applied broadly in the same way as for civil cases — save that usually it is done on a less precise basis and with less disclosure of detail. Also the ceilings on the income and capital limits are not applied. Anyone whose available funds do not exceed £75 if single or £120 if married, or who is on supplementary benefit, is automatically eligible. Anyone else however large his means is eligible if the court thinks that he requires assistance in meeting the costs he might incur. The fact that the means test is less severe than in civil cases is partly because in criminal cases the forms are filled out by the applicant and are not then scrutinised by experts, whereas in civil cases the Supplementary Benefit officials undertake a very exact inquiry into the applicant's means.

Legal aid for the juvenile court

Legal aid is available for proceedings in the juvenile court. If the proceedings are criminal, legal aid is subject to the ordinary rules of the criminal scheme. If the proceedings are civil, under the 1948 Children Act, the civil legal aid scheme applies. But all other civil proceedings, notably those in regard to care proceedings, are dealt with under the criminal scheme, because this is much speedier.

In care or criminal proceedings regarding children legal aid is granted to the child and there is normally no right for the parent to have it. (One exception, however, is where there is an unopposed application to revoke a care order. Under section 65 of the Children Act 1975, a parent can be given legal aid if the court makes an order that there is, or maybe, a conflict between the parent and the child. But this section of the 1975 Act had not been brought into force by 1981 and it must now be doubtful whether it will be in the foreseeable future.)

A statement of means for an applicant under 16 can be required from his parents. If the parent refuses to supply such a statement the court is still free to award legal aid. The parent can be asked to pay a contribution toward the costs — whether or not he has filled out the statement of means form.

Consequences of accepting an offer of civil legal aid

When an offer of civil legal aid is accepted, the applicant becomes liable to pay any contribution to which he has been assessed. Apart from this, however, he will not be required to pay anything further in regard to his own legal expenses even if the case in the end goes all the way to the House of Lords.

If he loses his case, he can be required to pay an amount towards the costs of his opponent. Normally this is fixed at the same figure as his own contribution payment. If his contribution is fixed at nil, he should therefore not have to pay anything towards his opponent's costs.

The charge

If he wins his case and recovers damages and costs, these are paid in the first instance into the legal aid fund which recoups itself first for the costs of the case. Only when these have been fully met is he entitled to any balance. In a very costly case which does not produce much in the way of damages, this could result in there being little or no balance to be paid to the successful legally aided party.

(c) *How to Apply for Legal Aid*

Applications for legal aid have to be presented to the appropriate authorities. It is usually advisable for the client to discuss the application with a solicitor and this can be done under the Legal Advice and Assistance Scheme (see p. 15 above). The solicitor will help the client fill in the forms. Social workers or Citizens' Advice Bureaux may also be willing to help in this way.

Application forms can be obtained from the Secretary of the Area Legal Aid Committee of the Law Society — the address would be obtainable from any local county court, Citizens' Advice Bureau or public library or in the telephone book under "Law Society." (The address of the Legal Aid head office is 29/37 Red Lion Street, London, WC2.). The CAB would normally also have forms. The forms should be sent to the Secretary of the Committee.

If the case is a criminal one, application must normally be made at the magistrates' court where the case is being heard. It can be made in the first instance orally but a form has to be filled in and signed. Requests for the form can be made by letter or telephone and it is desirable that an application be made at the earliest possible time. Again, however, it is always desirable for the client to discuss the completion of the form with a solicitor — especially in regard to the section in the form asking for Special Reasons why legal aid is sought. But a new form agreed in 1980 between the Law Society and the Justices' Clerks' Society should be in use in many courts. This asks the applicant to state whether he is in real danger of a custodial sentence or of losing his livelihood and puts directly the main other considerations which would influence a court in deciding whether to grant legal aid.

An applicant for legal aid is entitled to choose any solicitor who will take the case.

(d) *Appeal from Refusal of Legal Aid*

In civil cases, there is a right of appeal from the decision of the General Area Committee to an Area Appeal Committee.[3]

In criminal cases, there is no right of appeal, but one is entitled to reapply to the same court. Sometimes, where an applicant in person has been refused, a second attempt by a lawyer is more successful. If the case is going from the magistrates' court to the Crown Court and the magistrates have refused legal aid, a further application can be made to the Crown Court.

6. *COMPLAINTS AGAINST LAWYERS*

Complaining about Work

There are two main ways of complaining about a lawyer's work.

(1) *An action for negligence.* An action for negligence can only be sustained if the claimant can show that he has suffered loss through conduct by the lawyer which fell below the reasonable minimum professional standard. This is normally very difficult, particularly since most professional men tend to be reluctant to take up a case against a fellow member of the profession. Without the aid of a solicitor such a case is unlikely to succeed. Moreover, the courts have ruled that a lawyer, whether he is a barrister or solicitor, is immune from actions for negligence, however gross, if the negligence occurred in the course of advocacy. This would include also some part of the process of preparation of the court case, though it is uncertain where the line between work covered by the immunity and other work is drawn.

[3] This system replaced the previous system of Local and Area Committees on January 1, 1981. Local committees were abolished as an economy measure.

(2) *Complaint to the professional association.* Complaints against barristers should be sent to the General Council of the Bar, 11 South Square, Gray's Inn, London WC1R 5EL. Complaints against solicitors should be sent to the Law Society, 113 Chancery Lane, London WC2A 1LP, or to the Local Law Society.

If the complaint is one that can be pursued by an action for negligence the Law Society will inform the complainant that they cannot look into it.

Most complaints are rejected as unfounded. The complainant himself has no right to be represented or involved in the process of decision as to whether the complaint is well founded. He is simply informed at the conclusion of the inquiry as to the result.

If the client has been defrauded of money by a solicitor or his firm, the Law Society can pay compensation at its discretion out of the Compensation Fund. Apart from this, the only sanction available to the professional organisation is that of disciplinary action with the final threat of disbarment (barristers) or striking off the rolls (solicitors). These remedies do not directly aid the client.

If the complaint is against a solicitor and the client is not satisfied with the Law Society's handling of the matter, there is a final "court of appeal" in the person of the Lay Observer established by statute to oversee the complaints system. His office is in the Royal Courts of Justice, Strand, London WC2.

Complaining about the Bill

If the complaint is not about the lawyer's work but about the size of the bill there are also two methods of acting:

(1) *Review by the Law Society.* The Law Society maintains a free service in non-litigation matters whereby, *providing the bill has not yet been paid*, it considers and advises on the appropriateness of charges made by solicitors. If it considers that the charge is too high, it will order that it be reduced.

(2) *Taxation.* A client is always free to take the bill to court to be reviewed. If the work was in connection with a court case, the review would be by that court, if it was not in

a court case, the review would usually be by the High Court Taxing Office. The review (known as "taxation") can be sought even if the client has signed an agreement in advance with his solicitor for an agreed fee. But if the taxation results in less than one-fifth of the amount of the bill being reduced, the client has to pay the costs of the taxation. If he succeeds in getting more than one-fifth knocked off, the solicitor has to pay the costs of taxation.

3 The Courts System and Tribunals

To help a client with his legal problems may require some basic minimal grasp of the organisation of the courts system. The amount of information that needs to be mastered for most ordinary purposes is, however, not great.

1. *CIVIL AND CRIMINAL MATTERS DISTINGUISHED*

The first major distinction is that between civil and criminal matters, for there are courts that deal only with one or only the other, as well as some courts that do both. The difference between a civil and a criminal matter lies mainly in the nature of the remedy. Criminal cases end with a sentence of the court — of absolute or conditional discharge, or probation, or community service or a fine or some form of custodial penalty. A civil matter ends with a judgment or order of the court usually that the unsuccessful party pay damages or make other financial reparation to the winner, and in addition that he pay the winner's taxed costs. Sometimes, however, a civil case ends with an order that the loser stop doing something (such as molesting a wife), or do something (such as perform a contractual obligation).

The same facts can give rise to both civil and criminal proceedings. A typical example is a road accident, where the motorist to blame may be prosecuted for the crime of dangerous driving and also sued for the civil wrong of negligently causing the injury of another motorist or of a pedestrian. The criminal proceedings are usually brought by public agencies, notably, the police and the resulting penalty is not normally intended to provide any direct compensation to the injured person. A fine goes into public funds, not into the pockets of the injured party. (Criminal courts do, however, also possess some power to order the offender to make reparation directly to the victim.) But civil proceedings are launched by the private interests affected and are aimed to secure a direct remedy for a wrong.

Civil matters are dealt with primarily in the county court and the High Court; criminal matters are dealt with primarily in the magistrates' court and the Crown Court.

2. CIVIL CASES

(a) The High Court

The High Court is the superior or higher level of civil court. It is divided into Divisions each of which has a specialist character. The cases are heard by High Court judges all of whom have previously been practising barristers. The judge sits alone and is addressed as "My Lord." Juries are today virtually unknown in civil cases — though they occasionally occur in libel actions. Only barristers have a right of appearing as advocates.

The principal Division of the High Court is the Queen's Bench Division (QBD). This is the general Division dealing with ordinary actions in contract and tort. Most actions *started* in this Division are for debts. The great majority never reach trial because they are disposed of before this stage through payment or an agreed settlement or judgment without a contest. Most actions *tried* in the QBD are for compensation for personal injuries suffered in a road or factory accident. Libel and slander actions are also brought in the QBD. The Division has a highly specialised section dealing with collisions at sea (the Admiralty Court) and another that deals with commercial disputes, usually of a very substantial nature (the Commercial Court). The QBD sits in London in the Royal Courts of Justice in the Strand and throughout the country in the main provincial centres of population. (There are some 20 cities which have QBD courts either in permanent or frequent session.)

The second main Division of the High Court is the Family Division, formed in 1972 out of the rump of the disbanded Probate, Divorce and Admiralty Division. The Family Division deals with defended divorce cases, with maintenance and custody of children, guardianship, adoption, wardship, legitimacy. It also handles the ordinary probate transaction where there is no contest over a will. (Contested probate matters are the responsibility of the Chancery Divison.) The Family Divison, like the QBD, sits both in London in the Strand and throughout the country.

The third main Division of the High Court is the Chancery Division. Its main function is the traditional work of the Chancery Court — trusts, mortgages, settlements, charities, companies and partnerships. The Chancery Division functions primarily in London, though there are a few cities where it sits outside the capital.

In addition, the High Court has several even more specialised Divisons — notably the Restrictive Trade Practices Court, and the Bankruptcy Court.

High Court cases on the whole are somewhat costly and slow and tend to be ponderous in their procedure both before trial and at the trial. The proceedings are formal and it is rare for parties not to be legally represented.

(b) *The County Court*

The county court is the general, all-purpose court for smaller disputes. Its jurisdiction in actions for contract and tort from 1977 was limited to £2,000 - though an increase to £5,000 was being considered in 1981. The county court was established in 1846 as a small-man's court but the only sense in which the ordinary or small man has truly become the chief participant of the county court is as the defendant against whom the proceedings are brought. The judges are full-time professional judges, most of whom have previously been practising barristers. They are addressed as "Your Honour." In addition to the judge, there is the registrar, usually a solicitor, who has jurisdiction to try cases involving disputes of up to £200. Barristers and solicitors have an equal right of advocacy in the county court.

By far the largest single category of cases is that of action for debts — commonly of very small sums. Most of such cases are claims by department stores, mail-order companies and other large creditor organisations. Frequently they sell the claim at a discount to debt-collecting firms (such as British Debt Services Ltd.) which then make their profit by handling the claims in vast bulk. It has been estimated that British Debt Services Ltd. alone may handle as much as 40 per cent. of all county court actions. Other common actions in the county court are for damages for personal injuries, claims for broken contracts (say, against a builder or a central heating concern) and libel and slander actions.

If the claim is for under £2,000 both the High Court and the county court have jurisdiction, but if the case is started in the High Court, and reaches trial, the court has the power to order that it be removed to the county court.

As in the High Court, the overwhelming proportion of cases that are started in the county court never reach trial because they are disposed of at some earlier stage.

The county court also has an important jurisdiction in undefended divorce cases.

Another very significant jurisdiction is over possession and other types of action brought by landlords against tenants. As will be seen (see p. 67 below) with few exceptions no one may lawfully be compulsorily evicted unless the landlord has obtained a court order for possession.

A small number of county courts have been designated by the Lord Chancellor for the special jurisdiction of cases brought by the Commission for Racial Equality where it has failed to secure an acceptable settlement of a complaint (see further, p. 140 below).

County courts cases, by comparison with those in the High Court, are speedy and inexpensive. It is usually possible to get a case heard within some two to three months of starting it and there are far less in the way of pre-trial formalities. The actual hearing is also somewhat less formal and the atmosphere of the court less intimidating than in the High Court.

A recent innovation in the county court, designed to make it more available to the ordinary citizen, is the simplified and cheaper arbitration system for dealing with small claims (see further Chapter 14 generally).

(c) *Magistrates' Courts*

Although magistrates' courts are primarily concerned with criminal cases, they also have an important jurisdiction in certain civil cases. These are mainly claims for maintenance by deserted wives for the support of themselves or their children, or by mothers of illegitimate children for their support by the presumed fathers. There is also a right for

wives (or cohabitees) who are victims of violence from their
men to seek protection in the magistrates' court.

The main role of the magistrates' civil jurisdiction is to
dispose of the, usually extremely slender, resources of
defaulting husbands and fathers, many of whom have already
formed new liaisons with other women on whom, as often as
not, they have fathered new families. The civil function of
the magistrates' court is rarely put to use by any but the
poorest members of the community. Often it is a step on the
road to divorce; sometimes, however, no divorce is ever
obtained and the break-up of the marriage or of the relationship is never marked by any more formal act than the
magistrates' court order.

(d) *Appeals in civil cases*

Appeals from the High Court go as of right to the Court of
Appeal, Civil Division on a question of either fact or law.
Appeals from the county court go also to the Court of
Appeal, but no appeal lies on a question of fact unless the
amount in issue is more than £200. On a point of law an
appeal can be brought provided the amount in dispute is over
£20.

Appeals from the matrimonial jurisdiction of the magistrates' court go to the Divisional Court of the Queen's Bench
Division and from there to the Court of Appeal, Civil Division.

The Court of Appeal has the power to make any order that
could have been made by the first court.

Appeals from the Court of Appeal go to the House of
Lords, but only on a point of law of general public importance,
and only with leave.

3. *CRIMINAL CASES*

(a) *Crown Courts*

On January 1, 1972, the old system of assizes and quarter
sessions, which had existed for hundreds of years, was
abolished and replaced by the system of Crown Courts. The
chief difference between the two was that, whereas in the
assizes and quarter sessions, the judges processed from one
court to another, in the new system the court would sit

primarily in permanent session in the main centres of population. Mini-circuits still issue from the permanent regional courts, but to a far greater extent than before, the judges, court staffs and practitioners now remain fixed in a smaller number of locations.

The Crown Courts deal with all the most serious classes of criminal cases. They also deal with a variety of offences which can be dealt with either at the higher level or at the magistrates' courts level. The choice as to where one of such cases is heard lies variously with the prosecution, or with the defence or with the courts. From 1977, any offence triable either before a Crown Court or a magistrates' court gave the defendant the right to opt for trial at the higher level.

In approximately 60 per cent. of all cases in the Crown Courts, the defendant pleads guilty and the only question is what is the appropriate sentence. In the remaining 40 per cent. of cases, the defendant pleads not guilty and is tried by a court consisting of both judge and jury. The judge is a full-time or part-time professional, addressed as "My Lord." (If full-time, he is either a High Court judge or a Circuit judge; if part-time, he is called a Recorder. Recorders can be either barristers or solicitors; a solicitor Recorder is eligible for apppointment as a Circuit judge after three years on the bench.) The judge's function, apart from simply presiding, is to guide the jury as to the law and to sum up on the facts. The jury then arrives at its verdict. If this is guilty, the judge sentences the defendant.

The Crown Court also has a considerable number of cases committed for sentence only by magistrates. This occurs when the defendant elects to be tried or dealt with by magistrates but it turns out after he has been found guilty that in view of his record the magistrates' powers of sentencing are inadequate. They can then send him to the Crown Court for sentence.

Virtually all defendants in the Crown Courts are legally represented, normally under legal aid. Barristers, for the most part, have the monopoloy of the right of advocacy, but this is shared with solicitors in two types of cases -- first, on an appeal from the magistrates' courts; secondly, where the defendant has been committed for sentence only. There are also a small number of Crown Courts when for historical reasons solicitors enjoy a full right of audience.

(b) *Magistrates' Courts*

The vast majority of criminal cases are dealt with by the 700
or so magistrates' courts. They handle not merely the great
number of minor cases that fall outside the jurisdiction of the
Crown Courts, but also about 90 per cent. of all the cases
that could in theory be tried at the higher level.

Most of the country's 24,000 magistrates are unpaid,
mainly semi-trained laymen; but some 50 or so are full-time,
paid professionals (stipendiaries) who formerly were either
barristers or solicitors. All magistrates are addressed as "Your
Worship," or "Sir" (or "Madam"). The lay justices sit usually
in threes; the stipendiaries sit alone. The lay justices rely for
their knowledge of the law on their clerk, who increasingly is
a lawyer. The clerk, however, is not permitted to take any
part in the magistrates' decision-making on the facts.

(c) *The Juvenile Court*

Cases of children under the age of 17 are normally dealt with
by juvenile courts — magistrates' courts sitting in special,
private session. The bench for juvenile cases is specially con-
stituted from those who are thought to have particular com-
petence in this area and at least one must be a woman.

The press are allowed to be present but they cannot report
the child's name or address nor give any information which
could identify him or her.

The juvenile court can deal not only with defendants
charged with criminal offences but also with children said to be
in need of care and protection. For criminal cases the
jurisdiction of the court runs from age 10 to 17.

In the case of a child over 10 and under 14, however, there
is a presumption that a child under 14 does not know right
from wrong and therefore cannot be guilty of a criminal
offence. If, as is usually the case, the child is not represented
by a lawyer, this is a point worth bearing in mind. Positive
evidence must be given that he is capable of understanding
the nature of his act and that it was wrong. A child of low
intelligence might on this account legitimately be entitled to
be acquitted of the charge against him.

(d) *Appeals in Criminal Cases*

Appeals from the Crown Court go (normally on the grant of leave) to the Court of Appeal, Criminal Division. The appeal can be against conviction or sentence or both. The Court of Appeal is usually reluctant to quash a jury's verdict on the ground that it takes a different view of the evidence, but it should do so if it regards the verdict as "unsafe or unsatisfactory." The court can order that time spent appealing (up to 90 days) should be added on to the sentence — by way of deterrence of frivolous appeals.

Appeals from the magistrates' courts can go in either of two directions. If purely on a point of law, they can go to the Divisional Court of the Queen's Bench Divisions by way of Case Stated. If on law or fact, they can go to the Crown Court — sitting for this purpose without a jury.

The appeal to the Crown Court is by way of rehearing - which means that the evidence is all heard again from the start. This is different from the normal type of appeal where the evidence is taken from a written record of the first hearing — unless there is fresh evidence which was unavailable at the first trial.

After the case has been re-heard by the Crown Court it can go again by way of Case Stated on a point of law to the Divisional Court of the Queen's Bench Division.

Appeals from the Divisional Court and the Court of Appeal, Criminal Division lie only to the House of Lords, subject to a requirement that leave to appeal be obtained and that the court appealed from certify that a point of law of general public importance is involved.

4. *TRIBUNALS*

The tribunal system is complementary to that of the courts. Tribunals are specialist bodies each concentrating on one or another area of the law: supplementary benefits, national insurance, medical appeals, etc.

The chief difference between the methods of courts and those of tribunals is that the tribunal is supposedly more informal, quicker and cheaper. Each side pays its own costs, if any. Legal aid is not yet available for advocacy. Parties can usually be represented by a lawyer or non-lawyer, but save in those tribunals where trades unions play a large role, the ordinary citizen, more often than not, is unrepresented. Statistics show, however, that the person who is represented even if only by a friend or relative has a considerably greater chance of success than one who is not.[1] (Also the person who attends personally has a distinctly higher success rate than the one who does not.) Hearings come on much more rapidly than is common with civil courts. The rules of evidence are not normally strictly followed.

Procedure is usually left to a considerable extent to the chairman. The tribunal commonly consists of three members — one from each "side" and an impartial, often a lawyer, chairman.

Although by comparison with the ordinary courts, informality prevails, nevertheless, careful preparation and presentation are invaluable. Each side leads its evidence and challenges evidence of the other party with which it disagrees.

The decision does not have to be given in writing unless this is specifically asked for *in advance*. This is always worth asking for — simply so that the question of a possible appeal can be considered in the light of a full account of the decision to be appealed against.

The written notice of the decision normally states how an appeal can be made and the time limit within which appeals must be made.

[1] In the London area a very valuable function of providing representation is performed by the Free Representation Unit manned by young members of the Bar, Bar students and university law students. It handles many hundreds of cases without charge each year. It can be contacted at 3 Middle Temple Lane, London EC4, Tel: 01-353 3697.

4 Landlord and Tenant

Private tenancies of private landlords account for about 12 to 13 per cent. of the total number of living units in the country. About one-third are council tenancies. The remainder are owner-pccupied houses. Tenancies are therefore of considerable importance.

At a time of acute housing shortage, especially in areas of housing stress, it is often very difficult to obtain any premises at all. The housing shortage also has the effect of inhibiting even the tenant who knows his rights from exercising them, simply because he does not want to put his living accommodation at risk. But in spite of these difficulties, the tenant who knows the law is usually in a substantially better position than one who does not. Although the law may not be the only factor in the equation, it is often an important one. Armed with adequate understanding of the law or competent advice, the tenant can often win advantages or ward-off threats and so significantly improve his position.

The law in the field of landlord and tenant is immensely complicated and it is impossible in the space available here to do more than to indicate some of the basic concepts and to give some idea of the rules. For further reading on this topic see especially Martion Cutting, *A Housing Handbook* (Penguin, 1979) and two books published in the Social Work and Law Series by Sweet & Maxwell: Andrew Arden, *Housing Security and Rent Control* (1978), and Tom Hadden, *Repairs and Improvements* (1979). But note that the Housing Act 1980 has significantly altered the law, as will be explained here, and these books must be read subject to this qualification.

1. *THE STATUS OF THE OCCUPIER*

The status of the occupier of premises determines his legal

position and the degree of protection to which he is entitled
under the law. There are three basic categories that should be
established at the outset: tenants, licensees and trespassers.

A *trespasser* is easy to define since he has no right to be in
occupation and therefore enjoys virtually no protection at
law — except that even a trespasser cannot be evicted by
force save if he is removed from residential premises by the
dispossessed owner or by the officers of the law, the bailiff or
the under sheriff.

The difference between a *tenant* and a *licensee* is more
elusive. At the extremes there is no difficulty. A person who
has a written lease for five years at a fixed rent is obviously a
tenant; a friend who is allowed to use a house for the week-
end whilst the owner is away is equally obviously a licensee.
But at the margins the two concepts almost merge. Thus a
person can theoretically be a tenant even if he pays no rent -
though this is uncommon nowadays. On the other hand a
person can be a licensee even though he pays rent and has
exclusive occupation of at least part of the premises he
occupies - for instance someone who stays for a long period
in a hotel is not a tenant but he does have a contractual
licence. A licensee does not have full protection under the
Rent Acts, and may have no protection at all. Licensees
include such persons as a lodger, a friend allowed to live in
the house temporarily on payments of outgoings, or someone
staying in a house as an act of "grace and favour." But it has
always been said that a landlord cannot avoid the Rent Acts
applying by calling what is in reality a tenancy a licence and
that the courts will look at the real situation between the
parties.

The Court of Appeal in *Somma* v. *Hazelhurst* (1978)
appeared to weaken this doctrine when it gave effect to a
landlord's "non-exclusive occupation agreement" that was
patently designed to avoid the Rent Acts. An unmarried
couple sharing a double bed-sitter each signed an agreement
that neither had exclusive possession of the room and that, if
one left, the landlord could impose a new sharer on the
person remaining. The Court of Appeal held that there was
no evidence that the document was a sham and so refused to
give effect to the reality of the transaction. In a second case
in 1978 (*Aldrington Garages* v. *Fielder*) it took a very similar
line. Advisers to tenants were seriously concerned. But in two
other cases the Court of Appeal has shown that such alarm

may have been premature. In these cases (*O'Malley* v. *Seymour* and *Demuren and Adefope* v. *Seal Estates Ltd*,) the Court of Appeal rejected non-exclusive occupation agreements on the ground that they were either a sham or did not properly reflect the true agreement between the parties which was to enter a tenancy. In *Somma* and *Aldrington* the tenant was unable to discharge the burden of proof that the documents were mere shams. But if this can be shown, the Rent Acts will apply. (See (*LAG Bulletin*, June 1978, p. 138; April 1979, p. 87; and *New Law Journal*, October 16 and 23, 1980.) From the occupier's point of view it is greatly preferable to be classified as a tenant, since tenants generally have much better protection in respect of rent control and security of tenure.

Whether occupation is a tenancy or a licence therefore affects protection but so too does the type of tenancy and the type of licence. There are four main categories of tenants and several sub-categories. The main categories of tenants are: (1) Protected tenants. (2) Restricted tenants; (3) Secure tenants; (4) Shorthold tenants; and (5) Unprotected tenants.

Tenancies can be contractual or statutory. There are sub-tenancies and joint tenancies. Tenancies can be furnished or unfurnished.

Similarly, licences can be bare or contractual and, if the latter, can have a measure of restricted protection under the Rent Acts. But they can also acquire full security under the Housing Act 1980.

(1) *Protected tenants* hitherto have been the largest single class of private tenants - the normal category with maximum protection under the Rent Acts both in regard to the fixing of rent and in regard to security of tenure. Protected tenancies were formerly either *controlled* or *regulated*; the latter being either *contractual* or *statutory*.

Controlled tenancies were abolished from November 28, 1980 under the Housing Act 1980. From that date all controlled tenancies became regulated tenancies. In 1980 there were estimated to be some 200,000 such tenancies. The chief feature of controlled tenancies was their extraordinarily low rent fixed by reference to rateable values. They had to have been granted before July 1957 or have been renewed since that date on exactly the same terms or have been inherited once only by one family member from another. Every time a

new tenancy was granted the premises were de-controlled and
there were various other ways for landlords to get de-control.
The result of the conversion of all controlled tenancies to
regulated tenancies will be a considerable rise in their rents.

Regulated tenancies are tenancies where the rateable value
of the premises is under £1,500 in Greater London or £750
elsewhere. This covers all but luxury accommodation.

A regulated tenancy is *contractual* if it is running by virtue
of an agreement between landlord and tenant. It may be for a
fixed term - one year, two years, etc., - or it may be periodic -
e.g. weekly or monthly with no fixed limit. Most tenancies
are periodic. It makes no difference whether the tenancy is
written or oral.

A regulated tenancy is *statutory* if it exists not by agreement but by virtue of the Rent Acts. One common example
is where a contractual tenant stays on at the end of his fixed
term as he is normally entitled to do and pays rent at the
same rate as before. Another is where a periodic tenancy has
been brought to an end by a notice to quit which has expired.
A further form of statutory tenancy arises where the rent
officer has fixed an increased rent and a notice of increase
has been served on the tenant. Another instance is where the
tenant dies and a member of the family inherits the tenancy
(see p. 76 below).

Prior to 1974 there was an important distinction between
furnished and unfurnished premises — furnished tenancies
could not qualify for full protection as regulated tenancies.
But in 1974 this distinction was abolished and most furnished
tenancies became regulated tenancies. Similarly, prior to
1976 agricultural workers who occupied premises that went
with the job did not normally have protection under the
Rent Acts. But the Rent (Agricultural) Act 1976 changed
this and most such workers became regulated tenants.

(2) *Restricted tenants* are those who have only partial
protection under the Rent Acts, especially in regard to
security of tenure. Those in the category of restricted tenants
include:

(a) Tenants (furnished or unfurnished) who share essential
living accommodation, *e.g.* something more than a bathroom
or toilet, with their landlord.

(b) Tenants (furnished or unfurnished) whose tenancies
started after August 14, 1974 where there is a resident land-

lord - other than a purpose built block of flats. But a restricted tenant will be a protected tenant although there is a resident landlord if before the start of the present tenancy he had a protected tenancy, in the same or another part of the building.

(c) Furnished tenants with resident landlords whose tenancies started before August 14, 1974.

(d) Some licensees — those who have exclusive occupation of at least some part of their premises which falls short of giving them a tenancy. (Those in rooming houses are an example.) But such contractual licensees only have restricted contracts if they pay rent and get not only occupation but also furniture or services.

Restricted contracts or tenancies that existed prior to the coming into force of the Housing Act 1980 (August 1980) entitle the tenant to ask for security of tenure of up to six months from the rent tribunal and to have a reasonable rent fixed by the tribunal. Restricted contracts or tenancies that came into existence after August 1980 do not have these rights. In regard to security of tenure they are limited to a maximum of three months, obtainable if at all from the county court. In regard to rents they can still attempt to get a reasonable rent fixed by the tribunal but this is subject to the likelihood that by the time the rent has been reduced they will have been evicted by the county court.

(3) *Secure tenancies* were created by the Housing Act 1980. Previously it had been a matter of criticism that public sector tenancies were outside the protection of the Rent Acts. The 1980 Act establishes a form of protection for these tenancies which is very similar to that of the Rent Acts in regard to security of tenure though not in rent protection. Secure tenancies are those granted by local authorities, the Housing Corporation, housing trusts or charities, most Housing Associations (but not housing cooperatives), tenants of the new development corporations and of the Commission for New Towns. However there are a considerable number of exceptions including tenancies for a fixed period of more than 21 years; service tenancies; a person housed under some provisions of the Housing (Homeless Persons) Act 1977, until a year has passed; a person given accommodation specifically on a temporary basis whilst looking for somewhere to work in a new area (but after a year such a person becomes a secure tenant); a person not having a secure tenancy, who is given temporary accommodation whilst improvements are

made to his or her home; a letting to a student specifically stated from the outset to be to enable him to take up a course at a university or other institution of further education. But six months after the expiry of the course the student, if still there, would become a secure tenant.

One of the significant changes introduced by the 1980 Act in relation to council tenancies was to create a "tenant's charter" of terms and conditions implied by law out of which the parties cannot contract. Thus the tenant is allowed to take in lodgers (who need not be members of his family) without the consent of the landlord. A secure tenant can even create subtenancies of parts of his home — though only with the written consent of the landlord which consent cannot be unreasonably withheld. (Consent can however be reasonably refused if the result would be to create conditions of overcrowding.) Provisions about a requirement of written consent which is not to be unreasonably withheld apply also to improvements (see p. 57 below). Another feature of the "tenant's charter" is that local authorities are required now to publish a summary of the rules they apply for the allocation and change of accommodation and to maintain sets of such rules for public inspection and a summary for public distribution free of charge. (Under the 1980 Act the secure tenant also acquired a right to buy his council tenancy but this is not dealt with here.)

A tenancy can cease to be secure if it is assigned, or if the whole of the premises are sub-let (even if the sub-letting is with the consent of the landlord). The tenancy also ceases to be secure if during a fixed term the tenant dies and succession passes to someone who is not entitled to be a successor for the purposes of statutory succession. (The chief requirements are that the successor be either the spouse of the deceased or a close member of the family who has lived with the deceased during the 12 months prior to his death.) Only one succession is permitted.

(4) *Shorthold tenancies* likewise were created by the Housing Act 1980. But whereas secure tenancies could be seen as a victory for the tenants' lobby, shorthold tenancies are very much the reverse. It is said by many critics of the new concept that shorthold tenancies are an attempt by the Conservative Government to dismantle the whole Rent Act system. The Labour Opposition said during the passage of the Housing Bill through Parliament that it would abolish short-

hold tenancies when returned to power. The objective of shorthold tenancies according to the Conservative Government was to encourage landlords to rent for short periods without the fear that the tenant could not be removed if he proved unsatisfactory.

Shorthold tenancies can arise only after this part of the 1980 Act came into force in 1980. Nor can they affect a previous protected or statutory tenant if the new tenancy is given in respect of the same dwelling. But if a protected tenant accepts a new tenancy of premises that are different in any way the new tenancy could be a shorthold.

The definition of a shorthold tenancy is that (i) it is otherwise a protected tenancy, *i.e.* it would qualify as a protected tenancy were it not shorthold; (ii) it is for a fixed period of one year or more but under five years; (iii) the landlord cannot end the tenancy during that fixed term save for non-payment of rent or breach of some other obligation of the tenancy; (iv) before granting the tenancy the landlord has given the tenant a notice in specified form saying that it is to be a protected shorthold tenancy. and (v) either a rent for the premises is registered before the tenancy is granted or a certificate of fair rent is issued by the rent officer before the grant and, in that event, an application for registration of rent must be made within 28 days and not withdrawn and in the meanwhile the rent charged cannot be more than the figure stated in the certificate of fair rent. (A certificate of fair rent is one obtained by a landlord where the premises are empty and he plans to undertake improvements. He can ask the rent officer for a certificate as to what rent would be fair.) But both these last two requirements can be waived by the court if it thinks it "just and equitable." It remains to be seen what attitude the courts will adopt to this power.

Only the first fixed term will be capable of being shorthold. After that the tenancy becomes statutory or protected. Also the tenant (but not the landlord) can determine a shorthold tenancy during its currency by written notice of two months if the tenancy is for under two years and three months if it is between two and five years. This is so even if the contract denies such a right.

(5) *Unprotected tenancies* include the following:
(a) Those who occupy premises with rateable values out-

side the Rent Act limits. This applies solely to luxury accommodation.

(b) Those whose rent payment includes any bona fide element of board or a substantial attendance element such as room cleaning, changing the bed linen, etc. (See *LAG Bulletin*, March 1975, p. 73).

(c) Students who have tenancies from specified educational institutions — universities, polytechnics, teacher-training colleges and colleges of further education receiving grants from the D.E.S.

(d) Tenancies at a nil rent or a low rent. A low rent in this context means one that is less than two-thirds of the rateable value.

(e) Tenants of premises let genuinely for holiday purposes.

Sub-tenancies

A sub-tenancy arises when there are two levels of tenancy. The landlord has a tenant who in turn has a tenant. The sub-tenancy may be protected, restricted, shorthold, secure or unprotected depending on the circumstances. The chief problem created by sub-tenancies is when the intermediate tenancy (known as the mesne tenancy) comes to an end. This is considered below, see p. 74).

Joint tenancies[1]

If two or more persons take a tenancy together they may be joint tenants. This happens typically when people set up home together, each paying their share of the rent. Joint tenants are those who hold the property together as tenants. This is usually a stronger legal position than most other situations of flat or home sharers. Flat-sharers are not necessarily joint tenants. They may be mere licensees of one tenant or even licensees of the landlord. The correct legal description of the situation will depend on analysis of the actual facts of the case. Did the landlord negotiate with all the occupiers or only with one? Did he know the names of all or only one? Did he take up references of all or only of one? Is the rent book in one name or several? None of these facts

[1] See further A. Arden's book *op. cit.* (p. 35 above,) pp. 45-48

alone will be decisive; the true position usually has to be deduced from a number of facts.

If there is actually only one tenant and the rest are simply sharers there is no problem about one of the sharers leaving and another taking his place. But if the sole tenant departs, the others will be left without any legal interest in the premises or protection from eviction unless they can establish a new tenancy by paying the rent and having it accepted by or on behalf of the landlord.

If, on the other hand, there is a joint tenancy and one goes to be replaced by someone else, the landlord must actually agree to the new person explicitly or perhaps implicitly for him to become a joint tenant.

If the landlord enters into individual arrangements with each of the sharers and he controls the choice of a new person, he will probably avoid the impact of the Rent Acts. Again, if the rent varies with the number of occupants or if each tenant does not have the right to exclusive occupation of part of the premises it suggests that they are licensees rather than tenants. Conversely, if the rent is the same irrespective of the number of occupants, it suggests that they are joint tenants. From the tenants' point of view they are best advised to ask for one rent book between them, to pay rent in one sum for the whole of the premises and, if any of them leave, to pay the whole rent until a replacement occupier can be found. (See *LAG Bulletin*, November 1978, p. 265.)

In law, joint tenants are each fully liable for the whole of the rent and for all the liabilities of the tenancy. The landlord can, therefore, proceed against any or all of them. If one or more have left by the time that such action is taken, those remaining who are answerable to the landlord have a right to sue their former joint tenant for his share of the rent or other liability.

2. *LEGAL PITFALLS OF FINDING A PLACE TO RENT*

(a) *Accommodation Agencies' Fees*

It is now widely known that it is a criminal offence (under the Accommodation Agencies Act 1953) for an estate agent or accommodation agency to charge a prospective tenant for simply providing him with lists of places available.

The implication of a House of Lords decision in 1974 (*Saunders* v. *Soper*) is that agencies *can* validly claim their commission if the fee is payable only after the customer becomes a tenant and in consideration of the tenancy found through the agency. But if money is taken before an address is given or if a deposit is taken (even though it may be returnable when no tenancy results), or if money is taken after an address has been given and before the tenancy is taken, then in all these situations the fee is illegal under the Act, unless the agency can argue that it has provided some additional services.

If the charge is illegal, there are two separate consequences. One is the possibility of a prosecution. Few individuals will have the time, energy or resources to bring a private prosecution, and the police normally show a marked reluctance to take up such cases. But the local authority may be persuaded to take up the cudgels for local inhabitants.

The second question is whether the tenant can recover his payment. The answer in law is yes — even if he has signed an agreement to pay the amount in question. But obviously he is in a much stronger position if he has not yet paid. It is then for the agency to take action against him and, if he shows that he knows his rights and will put forward the defence of illegality, they are likely to drop the claim. If, however, he has already paid, its recovery will depend on whether the agency are prepared to disgorge. In all likelihood they will not do so — at least without a threat of prosecution — and it will then be for the tenant to take legal proceedings in the civil courts. (See pp. 170-171 below for the new procedure for small claims.)

(b) *Premiums*

At times of housing shortage the landlord will often be tempted to ask for a cash payment, in addition to rent, by way of premium or key money. If the premises in question are residential, such a demand is often illegal.

Money demanded by the landlord by way of security against non-payment of rent or against damage to the premises is permitted (under the 1980 Housing Act) provided it is not more than is reasonable having regard to the potential liability. But if the deposit exceeds one-sixth of the annual rent it is automatically a premium. Also if the tenant is asked (or required) to buy furniture or fittings, any inflated value put on the items is also an illegal premium.

Even a deposit can be an illegal premium. Each case depends on its own facts. A small amount to cover tenant's liabilities such as those for breakages would be legitimate. But if it appears to be for the purpose of securing the flat rather than for meeting genuine contingencies, it will be an illegal premium. In a 1976 case a company pleaded guilty to summonses under the Act where it had got a cash deposit of £200 against arrears of rent and damage to furniture. The court seemed influenced by the fact that the deposit was held purely for the benefit of the landlord. If it had been put on deposit and the interest held for the tenant the result might have been different.

There was one gap in the law — that it was not illegal for the incoming tenant to pay the outgoing tenant a premium, unless the landlord was in some way implicated. In 1976, however, the House of Lords held (in *Farrell* v. *Alexander*) that it was illegal for the outgoing tenant to demand a premium as a condition of a grant of a lease by the landlord.

If the prospective tenant refuses to pay, he will probably lose the possiblity of securing the premises. On the other hand, if he pays, he is at some disadvantage. But his position is considerably stronger than in the case of the commission paid to the accommodation agency *because he can deduct the illegal payments from his weekly or monthly payments of rent.* It is probably sensible however for the tenant to get advice before doing this. The offence of charging an illegal premium is one for which a prosecution would normally be brought, if at all, only by the local housing department. (See *LAG Bulletin*, 1975, p. 263).

(c) *Racial Discrimination*

A landlord may not normally discriminate on grounds of colour, race, ethnic or national origin in regard to the letting of premises. The only exceptions are where he or his family live on the premises and share accommodation with the tenants and either there are only one or two tenancies apart from his own or the premises consist of a boarding-house of six or fewer lodgers.

Anyone who believes himself to be the victim of racial discrimination can complain to the Commission for Racial

Equality, 10-12 Allington Street, London SW1, Tel:
01-828 2022. The Commission is not likely, however, to be
able to secure the tenancy for him. The best it is likely to be
able to achieve is to persuade or, if necessary, get the court
to compel, the landlord not to discriminate in future cases.
But under the 1976 Race Relations Act the victim of discrimination can take his own case to the county court (see further
p. 140 below). If the case goes to court, the complainant
might be rewarded damages.

3. *FIXING OR AGREEING THE RENT*

In private accommodation, rents are fixed by agreement, or
by law or by the rent-fixing authority.

For most privately rented accommodation, furnished as
well as unfurnished, the rent-fixing authority is the rent
officer, and on appeal, the rent assessment committee. For
those entitled only to restricted protection, it was formerly the
rent tribunal, but it is now the rent assessment committee —
acting as (and called!) the rent tribunal when exercising this
jurisdiction.

(a) *Rent Fixing for Controlled Tenancies*

The rent of controlled tenancies was fixed by law by
reference to the repairing obligations. If the tenant had
responsibility for the repairs the rent was four-thirds of the
gross rateable value of the premises as at November 7, 1956;
if the landlord was responsible for repairs the rent was twice
the rateable value.

When controlled tenancies became regulated tenancies
they were subject to much higher rents being fixed. But the
tenant was protected somewhat by two rules. One is the
phasing provisions for increases of rent — see p. 51 below.
The other is the rule that the rent cannot be agreed between
landlord and tenant alone — the new rent also has to be fixed
by the rent officer. A rent increase agreed between landlord
and tenant is not recoverable by the landlord. If the tenant
nevertheless pays such an increase he can recover two year's
worth of moneys so paid. As has been seen (p. 37 above),
the 1980 Housing Act provided for all controlled tenancies to

become regulated as from the date of commencement of that part of the Act — November 28, 1980.

(b) *Rent Fixing for Regulated Tenancies*

Regulated tenants have their rents fixed either by agreement between landlord and tenant or by the rent officer.

(i) *Rents fixed by agreement*

Assuming no rent has been registered, landlord and tenant can agree on a rent subject to certain statutory safeguards:

First, even a written agreement is not binding — either the tenant or the landlord (or the local authority) can go to the rent officer and ask for the rent to be reduced.

If the agreement is between a landlord and a tenant who already is in occupation as a protected tenant, the agreement is only enforceable by the landlord if it complies with the statutory requirements. These require that the agreement be in writing and signed by both parties. Also, the agreement must bear a notice at its head in characters no less conspicuous than those used in any other part of the document. The notice must state that the tenant's security of tenure cannot be prejudiced if he fails to enter into the agreement and that the agreement does not deprive either party of his right to apply to the rent officer for the rent to be fixed.

But if the rent has not been registered, the rent will be that agreed between landlord and tenant, until one or other or both of them refer it to the rent officer.

If the tenancy is a "statutory" one (p. 38 above) and no rent has previously been registered the rent payable is the last rent agreed. The landlord cannot normally increase the rent without application to the rent officer. However there are certain exceptions:

Increases without application for registration - The landlord can increase the rent in regard to increases in rates and in services provided. In each case he must give a valid Notice of Increase to the tenant and the increases are phased (see p. 51 below). The period of claims in arrear is limited. Previously there was also power to increase the rent in respect of improvements made by the landlord. This has been abolished

by the Housing Act 1980 where there is no registered rent. If
the landlord makes improvements he will therefore have to
obtain a registered rent if he wishes to increase the rent.

(ii) *Rents fixed by the rent officer*
Either party or the local authority can ask the rent officer
to register a "fair rent."

The *"fair rent"* concept was introduced into the law by
the 1965 Rent Act. It is fixed by the rent officer on the basis
of what is right for those premises having regard to their size,
nature, condition and situation and to rents for comparable
properties in the area.

The Rent Act 1974, which made most furnished premises
protected, and therefore brought them into the fair rent
system, required the rent officer to have regard also to the
state of the furniture provided, subject to deterioration
caused by the tenant and his family or lodgers.

But in fixing the fair rent the rent officer is supposed to
ignore any value attributable to the scarcity of that kind of
accommodation in the district. The rent officer should also
ignore new amenities in the area unless the landlord provided
or paid for them. In most areas the rent officers have
developed rules of thumb for fixing rents — so much an
average-size room or so much per square foot. The process is
much influenced by "comparables" or the levels of rent for
other similar properties in the area. A register is kept at the
local rent office.

If no rent has been registered the landlord or tenant or
both or the local authority can apply to have one registered
at any time — even if they have only just concluded an agreement on the rent to be paid. In other words, if the tenant
thinks or is told that he is being overcharged he can apply to
the rent officer immediately after he takes possession. Nor
can such action by a protected tenant result in a lawful
eviction. Whether it is wise to apply for the rent to be fixed
depends on the existing rent in relation to local values. The
rent officer may be willing to offer informal guidance. One
can inspect the register at the rent office, but interpretation
of the information in the register requires some specialised
local knowledge.

If the tenant applies for the rent to be fixed, he has to
complete a simple application form on which he must fill in
the rateable value of his premises and the rent he thinks
should be fixed. The form can be obtained from the rent

officer, who will also normally advise on how to fill it in. The proposed rent must be entered, even if the tenant does not know what it should be — this is a technical requirement without which the application is defective. The amount entered by the tenant will not, however, necessarily have any influence on the rent officer.

The rent officer will give the landlord an opportunity of stating his view and will then fix a date to come to see the premises. The whole process is usually very informal and it costs nothing unless either side chooses to employ a surveyor, lawyer or other expert. Any such costs are borne by the party employing the expert.

If the rent fixed seems too high, either side can appeal to the rent assessment committee within 28 days. But until the appeal is decided the tenant has to pay the new rent. The new rent applies from the date of the registration — it used to be the date of the application but this was changed by the 1980 Housing Act. If there is an appeal the rent fixed by the committee takes effect from the date of the committee's decision.

The rent assessment committee consists of a lawyer chairman and two others, often surveyors or valuers. Both sides to the appeal are provided with lists of the comparable rents taken into account by the rent officer. If the appeal is to have any chance of success it will be necessary to show that these are inappropriate. For this purpose it is desirable to be able to show that the properties referred to by the rent officer are different as to size, age, situation, amenities, etc.

A surveyor's or valuer's evidence is extremely desirable. In London help to obtain such professional assistance is available through the Surveyor's Aid Scheme through the local Citizens' Advice Bureau.

In general it is fair to say that the rent assessment committees tend to set rents higher than rent officers. The reasons are unknown but it means that an appeal against the decision of a rent officer is not normally in the tenant's interests.

The effect of registration. Once a rent has been fixed by the rent officer it becomes the registered rent which is the maximum rent obtainable until it is either increased by a new registration or is cancelled or the increase is on account of services, rates or improvements (see below).

It is not a criminal offence to charge a protected tenant

more than the registered rent but the tenant can recover any
unlawful increase for two years back either by legal action or
by deducting the amount from rent due. (The period is one
year when the rent is irrecoverable because of a failure to
comply with the rules laying down the formalities required in
rent agreements.) However before deciding that the tenant is
being overcharged it is worth bearing in mind that the
registered rent is exclusive of rates whereas rent is usually
fixed and paid inclusive of rates. Check this point by deducting the rate element in the actual rent.

Increasing a registered rent

(a) *New registration* — in the normal way application for a
new registration will come from the landlord. Most registered
rents are increased on reconsideration after the lapse of some
years. Normally the registration lasts for at least two years. It
used to be three years but this period was reduced to two by
the Housing Act 1980. But a transitional rule provided that
the three year period continues to be applicable where there
was already a rent registered. In that case the two year period
applies only after the *next* application.

(b) *Cancellation* — landlord and tenant can apply to the
rent officer jointly to have the registration cancelled and a
new fair rent fixed before the lapse of the normal two year
period. This is very rare. Such an agreement must be in
writing and must state that the tenant's security of tenure is
unaffected and that the tenant can still apply to the rent
officer to have the rent fixed in spite of the agreement. It
must also state that a registered rent which results in an
increase is subject to phasing (see p. 51 below).

A second type of cancellation within the two year period
is where there have been such substantial changes in the
terms of the tenancy, the condition of the premises or
furniture that the registered rent is no longer fair. Either
party can then apply to have the rent reviewed. In practice
however this is likely to help landlords more than tenants
since any decrease in value as a result of the change will
normally be more than outweighed by an increase in value
due to inflation.

A third type of cancellation, introduced by the 1980
Housing Act, is where two or more years have elapsed since
the last registration and there is no regulated tenancy at

present the landlord can apply to have the registered rent cancelled. The effect is that he can then charge a higher rent to an incoming tenant. Previously, the new tenant would have had the benefit of a registration made in the time of some previous tenant.

(c) *Charges for services, rates or improvements*
Services — a landlord can increase his rent if the cost of providing any services or furniture has gone up. He need not apply to the rent officer for permission to make such an increase providing the rent officer agreed at the time of the registration that the services element in the rent should be variable and on what basis. Nor need the landlord serve a Notice of Increase on the tenant — though as has been seen, he must do so if no rent has been registered.

Rates — the landlord is entitled to increase his rent to take account of rises in the rates attributable to those premises. He need not apply to the rent officer nor need he serve a Notice of Increase — though again he must serve such a notice if there is no rent registered. An increase on account of rates can only be backdated six weeks however.

Improvements — if the landlord carries out improvements (as opposed to simple repairs) he can increase the rent by 12½ per cent. per year of their costs. No backdating is allowed. A Notice of Increase is required whether or not the rent is registered.

Phasing of increases

Where a rent is registered and this results in the rent being raised, the increase must normally be phased. This does not apply, however, where a tenancy is granted after registration to a new tenant. Nor does it apply to increases due to better services or rates but it does apply to increases due to improvements.

Phasing can now be spread only over two years. Formerly, the method was to take one third of the increase or 40p, whichever was the greater. This was the increase payable in the first year. In the second year, two-thirds or 80p whichever was more, was payable and in the third year the balance was paid. The Housing Act 1980 altered the system in respect

to increases taking effect after the commencement of this
part of the Act (November 1980). There is now no minimum
increase and phasing is to spread over two rather than three
years with half being claimable in each year.

(c) *Rent Fixing for Restricted Tenancies*

The rent is fixed in the first instance by agreement between
landlord and tenant. Hitherto, if either party wished, application could be made to the rent tribunal for a reasonable rent
to be fixed and once this was fixed it became a criminal
offence to charge more. The Housing Act 1980 altered the
system by abolishing the rent tribunal and giving the function
of fixing rents for restricted tenancies to rent assessment
committees. To confuse matters however the committee
when sitting to determine rents of restricted tenants will be
called a rent tribunal.

For restricted tenancies arising pre-August 1980 rents can
still be referred to the rent assessment committee and such
committee can still give security of tenure for up to six
months. But for restricted tenancies arising after August
1980, the 1980 Act has totally changed the position by
restricting the maximum security of tenure to three months
and by requiring an application for security of tenure to be
considered by the county court rather than by the rent
tribunal. It will therefore normally be pointless for a restricted
tenant to apply for a reasonable rent to be fixed since the
result could be a notice to quit and a possession order from
the county court.

If a rent is registered however the same rules apply as to
regulated tenancies so that an application for a new rent
cannot normally be made for two years. Also, as with
regulated tenancies a registered rent can be cancelled on
application by the landlord if not less than two years has
elapsed since the last registration and the dwelling is not
subject to a restricted tenancy at the time of the application.

(d) *Rent Fixing for Secure Tenancies*

The system of fixing rents for local authority tenants was not
changed by the 1980 Housing Act. The rent is fixed by the
council and is brought to the attention of the tenant in a

notice which must give at least four weeks warning. Although in theory it is possible to challenge such raises in rents in the courts on the ground that they are not reasonable, in practice such challenges are normally doomed to failure.

The Housing Act 1980 provides that rents of secure tenants are not to be increased on account of any lawful improvements made by the tenant. Moreover where the improvement has been made with the written consent of the landlord, he can reimburse the tenant to the extent that the landlord thinks appropriate when the tenant leaves.

(e) *Rent Fixing for Shorthold Tenancies*

As has been seen (p. 41 above) the basic premise is that the rent for shorthold tenancies will be registered after being fixed by the rent officer or, on appeal, the rent assessment committee. If the rent is not already registered when the tenancy commences, application for registration must be made within 28 days and not withdrawn. However the 1980 Act gives the courts the power to waive this requirement and this could be an important escape hatch for landlords. Where no rent has been registered the tenant is of course always entitled to apply for the rent to be fixed.

(f) *Rent Fixing for Unprotected Tenancies*

Tenancies that are unprotected are not subject to any legal rules controlling the rent fixing process. The rent is simply a sum agreed between landlord and tenant.

4. *RENT AND RATE REBATES AND ALLOWANCES*

Rent rebates (for council tenants) and rent allowances (for private tenants) are available to help rent payers with insufficient means. This is an extremely important welfare benefit. The scheme applies equally to furnished, unfurnished, protected and unprotected tenancies. It even applies to boarders, sharers, lodgers, students, occupants of hostels - in fact to virtually anyone who is paying for the use of premises as a home. Anyone on supplementary benefit will normally qualify to have the rent paid as part of the supplementary benefit (see below). The schemes are run by local councils to whom applications must be made. Many people do not apply because they wrongly think they are earning too much to make them eligible.

The actual process of calculating whether a person is entitled to a rebate or allowance is not simple. The Town Hall should be consulted for information as to whether one qualifies.

The rebate or allowance is given for six months (pensioners get it for one year), at the end of which the tenant must reapply. Any changes of income must be notified to the council.

The rebate is paid by way of deduction from the weekly rent. Rent allowances are paid by cheques, postal orders or other means convenient to the tenant.

An authority can depart from the model scheme providing no tenant receives less rebate or allowance as a result. There will therefore be minor variations in the scheme from area to area. It is important for advisers to consider the applicability of the scheme to cases. Nor should it be assumed that the calculations done by the local council are necessarily correct. An appeal can be lodged within 28 days, by writing to the authority which made the determination.

Rebates are also available in respect of rates. Those who qualify for rent rebates or allowances will normally be eligible for rate rebates too. The council will explain the method of calculation. Application forms should be available from the local authority's treasurer's department. Usually it will be possible to apply for a rent and rate rebate on the same form.

Those on supplementary benefit do not qualify for rent or rates rebates or allowances because their entitlement to supplementary benefit is calculated to give them a "rent element." A problem occurs however when the rent paid is regarded as higher than is reasonable. If this creates financial difficulties a social worker can sometimes play a valuable role in persuading the supplementary benefit authorities to use their discretion in favour of the tenant. It is also worth noting that those on supplementary benefit who are also in receipt of a national insurance benefit such as a retirement pension or widow's benefit, or who have any other regular income, may be better off if they do not claim supplementary benefit but claim rent rebate allowances and rate rebates instead. For guidance as to whether a person qualifies for rent and rates rebates and allowances consult the local council, or a Citizens' Advice Bureau, Housing Aid Centre, the Child Poverty Action Group or Shelter.

5. *THE RENT BOOK*

Anyone who pays rent weekly, whether his tenancy is furnished or unfurnished, is legally entitled to a rent book which must give the details of the tenancy and of the tenant's rights. Failure to provide a rent book is a criminal offence and should be reported to the housing department of the local authority. Council tenants are given a rent book or rent card.

The absence of a rent book or other written document does not, however, mean that the tenant can be turned out on the ground that there is no lease. An oral agreement together with occupation and payment of rent is sufficient to give the tenant the rights of a tenant.

Entries in the rent book are, however, evidence of the tenant's status (as a furnished or unfurnished tenant) and of the payment or non-payment of rent. Entries (or blanks) can be challenged by either side if they are inaccurate.

6. *THE LANDLORD'S IDENTITY*

The Housing Act 1974 gives the tenant the right to have the landlord's name and address and to be informed if the landlord assigns his interest to someone else. Any tenant or sub-tenant of residential accommodation can write to the immediate landlord or to the person who has demanded rent or to any agent of the landlord, asking for written details of the landlord's name and address. He must receive them within 21 days of the receipt of the letter. If the landlord is a company the tenant can also ask for the name and address of every director and of the secretary of the company.

Failure to comply is a criminal offence, the maximum penalty for which is a fine of £500. Prosecution must be by the local authority. Information about the alleged offence should be given to the Tenancy Relations or Harassment Officer of the council.

When a landlord assigns his interest, the new landlord must give tenants notice of the fact within two months and must furnish his name and address. Again, failure to do so is a criminal offence with a maximum penalty of a £500 fine.

7. *PAYING THE RENT*

The tenant is under an obligation to continue to pay the rent. If for any reason the landlord makes this impossible by refusing to accept rent, the tenant should continue to offer it on each weekly or other due date. If refused, the money should be put aside, preferably in a Post Office Savings account or other safe place, so that it is available if and when the landlord again signifies willingness to receive it. It is best to write to the landlord (keeping a copy) stating that the money has been offered.

The tenant should get the rent book filled in each time he pays his rent, to provide evidence of payment. If the landlord refuses to acknowledge payments in this way, the tenant could ask the housing department of the local authority to intervene on his behalf.

8. *THE TENANT'S RIGHT TO ENJOY QUIET POSSESSION*

In return for his agreement to pay the rent, the tenant is entitled to what the law calls quiet enjoyment of his premises. This means that the landlord must not do anything that in practice prevents his getting the benefit of the lease.

If the landlord does anything to interfere with the tenant's right to quiet enjoyment which falls short of eviction or attempted eviction the tenant's remedy is to take proceedings in the county court for an injunction and/or damages. If he becomes the victim of an unlawful eviction or of acts designed to cause him to leave his home he can equally go to the county court for an injunction and/or damages and can also put in motion criminal proceedings for unlawful eviction or harassment. Both types of proceedings by the tenant against the landlord in the county court or the magistrates' court are dealt with at pp. 77-78 below.

9. *REPAIRS*[2]

(a) *Improvements by the Tenant*

The Housing Act 1980 provides that in secure tenancies, protected tenancies and statutory tenancies whether starting before or after the Act a new term is to be implied that the tenant will have to get the landlord's written consent to make improvements. An improvement for these purposes means any alteration in or addition to the property and includes in the case of secure tenancies external decoration. However the Act also provides that consent is not to be unreasonably withheld by the landlord. Any dispute between landlord and tenant can be resolved by a decision of the county court. The effect of this new rule therefore is that the tenant can now make improvements providing he gets consent from either the landlord or the county court. Improvements would not lead to an increase in rent since improvements made by the tenant have to be ignored by the rent officer when deciding on a fair rent. One possible advantage of making improvements is that it could be a factor to be taken into account by a court if it has to decide whether it is reasonable to give the landlord a possession order.

The tenant may be able to get a grant from the local authority to help pay the cost of improvements. Previously it was necessary to show that one was either the owner of the premises or had at least five years left on a lease to get a grant. But applications can now be received from most tenants.

(b) *Getting the Landlord to do Repairs*

The landlord's duties to repair may arise out of the contractual relationship between himself and the tenant or by operation of law, irrespective of what he has agreed. If there is a written contract, this should be looked at to see what, if anything, it says about repairs. Commonly, it will say little or nothing about the landlord's duties in this regard. In this situation, or

[2] See further especially Tom Hadden, *Housing Improvements* (Sweet & Maxwell, 1979).

in the situation where there is no written contract at all, the tenant will have to rely on obligations implied by the law.

The most important of these is the duty to repair the structure, exterior and water, sanitary, electrical and gas installations. This duty arises under section 32 of the 1961 Housing Act. (See *LAG Bulletin*, July 1977, pp. 156-159.) It could be invoked, for instance, if the toilets in the premises get blocked, the electrical system is faulty, the ceiling falls in or there is rising damp. The duty applies to any lease (including council tenancies) for less than seven years which started after November 24, 1961. It therefore applies to any tenancy for an indefinite period (weekly or monthly or from year to year) or for a tenancy for a fixed period provided it is under seven years.

The duty can be avoided only with permission of the county court. Any attempt to get the tenant to agree to waive his rights under section 32 is therefore legally ineffective.

A tenant who moved in before November 24, 1961 cannot claim the benefit of the 1961 Act unless he can argue that there is a new tenancy after that date or, in some cases, if there has been a written rent agreement in which the landlord has accepted liability under section 32 of the Housing Act 1961. (This is common on conversion from controlled to regulated tenancies.) The tenant can only rely on the basic rule that, unless there is anything in the agreement to the contrary, the landlord is responsible for repairs to the exterior and structure of the building and for keeping common parts of the building (stairs, passageways, roofs, gutters, etc.) in reasonably safe condition.

A landlord is normally responsible for injuries caused by his failure to repair the common parts of the building, including the roof and gutters. The House of Lords ruled in 1976 (in *Liverpool City Council* v. *Irwin*) that a landlord (including a local authority) owes his tenants an implied duty to take reasonable care to maintain the common parts, *i.e.* stairs, lifts and the lighting on the stairs, in a state of reasonable repair and efficiency.

If the tenancy is furnished, there is an implied undertaking that it is for for human habitation at the time when the tenancy starts. The same duty exists in relation to houses let unfurnished at a very low rent. But the duty to see that premises are fit for human habitation does not include a duty to *keep* in repair.

Where the landlord and the tenant share facilities such as a kitchen or w.c., the tenant has a legal right to complain if the shared facilities are not kept in repair.

One important rule is that the landlord only becomes liable for repairs if and when he has been informed of the defect. The tenant must therefore inform him of anything which needs doing - including any suspected defects which require investigation. Ideally, this should always be done in writing and a copy kept.

The rule requiring notice to the landlord is very strict. The House of Lords decided in 1973 that where the defect is a latent one not known to the tenant and where, therefore, by definition, the tenant cannot give notice of it to the landlord, the landlord is not liable for the repairs. In that case the tenant and his wife were not able to recover damages when the bedroom ceiling collapsed on them at night causing injuries. It is therefore vital that tenants take the trouble to inspect their own premises regularly and report any actual or suspected faults to the landlord.

On the other hand, a landlord can have notice of a defect through the actual or even the implied knowledge of his own employees. A council was held liable in 1973 to pay damages for the flooding of a council house after the tenant had called the plumber to look at his water tank. The plumber noticed that the tank was discoloured through corrosion but did nothing about it. The Court of Appeal held that the council was responsible because the plumber ought to have realised that repairs were needed.

The tenant's remedies against the landlord are either to sue him for damages or to invoke the law to get the repairs done or both.

To sue for damages, court proceedings must be started, usually in the county court. (See "Actions in the County Courts," p. 164 below). This has the disadvantage that it may cost money and may take a while, but, if the tenant qualifies for legal aid, may nevertheless be worth attempting. The damages will be assessed on the difference between the value of the tenancy to him as it is and as it should be. He will also be able to recover for any loss or damage to his own property (for instance, through damp) or for inconvenience (say, through the non-usability of the toilet for a period of weeks) or discomfort or loss of enjoyment.

But an action for damages will not itself get the repairs done. To achieve this he can either go to court or he can do the repairs himself and deduct the cost from the rent.

An order from the court requiring the landlord to do the repairs (known as an order of specific performance) is not available as of right but it may be obtained in a case where the failure to do the work is serious from the point of view of the tenant's enjoyment of his tenancy.

Normally, there is no right to withhold rent simply because the landlord has failed to do the repairs. But if the tenant does the repairs himself then he can recover the reasonable costs of such repairs by deduction from the rent or even out of accumulated arrears of rent. Notice of the defect must, however, have been given to the landlord. He should be warned that if he fails to do the repairs, the tenant intends to do them himself and to deduct the cost from the rent. The builder's estimate should then be sent to the landlord with sufficient opportunity for the landlord to challenge the estimate or to get an alternative quote.

If the landlord attempts to sue for possession on the grounds of the tenant's non-payment of rent, the tenant would enter a defence based on the repair-it-yourself doctrine (established in the case of *Lee-Parker* v. *Izzet* [1971] 1 W.L.R. 1688 and confirmed in *British Anzani (Felixstowe) Ltd.* v. *International Marine Management (U.K.) Ltd.* [1979] 2 A.E.R. 1063). A way of heading-off such action would be to go to the county court before carrying out the repairs, to get the court to make a declaration that the tenant is entitled to go ahead to make the repairs and deduct the reasonable costs from the rent. (See further S. Sedley, *LAG Bulletin* (1973), p. 173; (1974), p. 161; and A. Arden *ibid.*, (September 1979), p. 210.)

Obviously, however, the only repairs that are covered by this doctrine are ones for which the landlord is responsible. The landlord should in any event be given notice of the intention to carry out the repairs and be given a reasonable time to do the work himself. A tenant thinking of taking advantage of the rule might be well advised to consult a lawyer or at least a Citizens' Advice Bureau to check that the repairs in question are included in the landlord's legal duty to repair.

(c) *Getting the Council to Intervene*

There are two main sources of powers for local authorities - under the Public Health Acts and under the Housing Acts.

The Public Health Acts are less wide in their provisions and in the situations in which they can be invoked.

Public Health Acts

A local authority has power to deal with "statutory nuisances" which means any circumstances in a building which are "prejudicial to health or a nuisance." This includes such conditions as leaking roofs, damp, broken windows, rotten woodwork, blocked toilets, dangerous ceilings, defective wiring and even faulty window sash-cords. (Defective decoration is not covered.)

If any such condition exists, it should be reported to the local public health inspector. He will serve an abatement notice on the landlord (under s. 93 of the Public Health Act 1936) requiring him to put the matter right. If this is not done, the local authority *must* issue a summons in the magistrates' court, which can result in an order requiring the work to be done or a fine or, if the house if unfit for human habitation, a closing order. This power is widely used.

If this procedure would be too slow or if the landlord cannot be found, or if the landlord has ignored a court statutory nuisance order, the local authority can do the work itself after giving due notice to the landlord under Public Health Act 1961, S. 26.

Alternatively, a private individual aggrieved by a statutory nuisance can take the landlord to the magistrates' court under section 99 of the Public Health Act 1936. (See *LAG Bulletin*, 1977, pp. 156-159.) This is now used a good deal against both local authorities and private landlords. The procedure is first to write requesting the work to be done and if this fails to lay an information at a magistrates' court. Forms are available from the courts, but they do not have to be used. In fact, it is not necessary that the information be laid in writing. The statement must give the name of the complainant, his address and the allegation. The complaint must be made within six months of the offence. The court must then decide whether to issue a summons. The maximum penalty is a £20 fine plus an order for compensation to the complainant if he can show that he has suffered damage. A successful complainant can be allowed his costs as part of the court's order. The court can order a local authority to abate a nuisance created by a private landlord.

Where the defect concerns lavatories, drains, soil, pipes and sewers, the local authority has even more specific powers and duties. There is a duty on the local authority to see that the installations exist in proper order, that repairs are done and that replacement and further installations are made where necessary. Any problem with these installations should therefore be drawn to the attention of the public health inspectors.

The Public Health Acts apply to all types of premises whether privately or council owned, rented or owner occupied. They also apply even if the premises have been found to be so unfit as to justify demolition.

Housing Acts - 1957, 1961, 1964, 1969, 1971, 1974, 1980

Where a house is so defective as to be *unfit for human habitation*, the local authority has a duty to take action. The standard of unfit for human habitation is a low one. The public health inspectors will be able to advise whether the house does or does not qualify.

If the local authority proves recalcitrant, the tenants are entitled to ask the magistrates' court to complain to the medical officer of health. Section 157 (2) of the Housing Act 1957 says that a justice of the peace may complain to the medical officer of health that a house is unfit for human habitation. It then becomes the duty of the medical officer for the area to inspect the property and to report to the local authority. This procedure has been used a good deal in recent years.

If the house is beyond repair at a reasonable cost, the local *must* serve a notice on the landlord requiring him to do the necessary repairs. (See *LAG Bulletin*, October 1978, p. 234). If he fails, the local authority may itself do them and charge the owner with the costs (1957 Act, s. 10). The person on whom the notice is served has the right to appeal within 21 days to the county court. The court has a wide discretion as to whether to confirm or quash or vary the notice.

If the house if beyond repair at a reasonable cost, the local authority has a number of options. It can first ask the landlord either to put the house into a proper state or to cease using it for occupation. Secondly, it can compulsorily purchase the property and patch it up for short-term use. Thirdly, it can issue a demolition order. Fourthly it can make a closing order. In any of these circumstances, the tenant will lose his tenancy, though in the case of a demolition or closing order or an undertaking by the landlord not to use, the local authority has a duty to rehouse the occupants under the Land Compensation Act 1973. Depending on the length of residence the local authority may also have a duty to compensate them. For both reasons local authorities are usually reluctant to invoke these powers and prefer to exercise the power of compulsory purchase - or do nothing.

If the house is *not unfit for human habitation*, the local authority can serve a notice on the landlord (under the Housing Act 1957, s. 9 (1) (*a*) requiring the landlord to make repairs to bring it up to a reasonable standard. If the landlord defaults, the local authority can do the work itself. A section 9 order has to be approved by a committee and this usually involves delays. The landlord incurs no penalty if he refuses to comply. Moreover, often the local authority lacks the resources and/or the will to use its default powers. A new power for local authorities to serve repair notices on landlords was included in the Housing Act 1980. This can be done only at the request of an occupying tenant on the basis that the premises though not technically unfit for human habitiation are in such a condition as to interfere materially with the tenant's personal comfort.

Special rules apply if the house is in *multiple occupation*, *i.e.* where a house is occupied by persons who do not form a single household. The special rules give the council extra powers, even where the premises are not technically overcrowded.

If a house in multi-occupation is badly managed — drains blocked, rubbish in passageways, dirty kitchens, etc. — the local authority can require the person who collects the rent (the manager) to follow the management code (laid down in the Housing (Management of Houses in Multiple Occupation) Regulations (1962). This requires standards of good management in relation to repair, maintenance, cleaning and good order of communal facilities. (See *LAG Bulletin*, February 1978, p. 34.) Breach of the code can be punished by a fine in the magistrates' court. It can also lead to a control order (see below) or to an order under section 14 of the Housing Act 1961.

A section 14 order specifies the work to be done to put the house into a proper state. If the manager fails to carry it out, the local authority may do so. Failure constitutes an offence.

A local authority can also order a landlord to remedy basic shortcomings in the building which make it unsuitable for the number of households living there. This could apply, for instance, to a lack of adequate lighting, heating, ventilation, washing facilities, toilets, etc. The landlord has the right to appeal to the county court against the making of such an order. If it is confirmed and the landlord does not comply (under section 15 of the 1961 Act), the local authority may do the work itself.

A control order permits the local authority either to compulsorily purchase or to take over the running of a house in multiple occupation. It can be made where thought necessary for the safety, welfare and health of the people in the house under section 73 of the 1964 Act.

Local authorities have extensive powers to acquire property in a variety of circumstances by agreement or compulsorily. They may buy property, if necessary, by compulsory purchase to complete improvement of an area where owners are unable or unwilling to repair their own properties.

They can also strengthen their powers by declaring special housing areas. If they declare a *housing action area* (under Part IV of the 1974 Housing Act) they obtain special powers to rehabilitate premises and to undertake slum clearance. They also get extra powers to make generous (75 per cent. to 90 per cent.) grants to owners for repairs and improvements. If they declare a *general improvement area* (under Part II of the 1969 Housing Act and Part V of the 1974 Housing Act) as amended by the Housing Act 1980, they obtain special powers to compel owners to rehabilitate and to compulsorily purchase property, plus additional powers to make grants to owners for repair and improvement. (For details see a valuable series of articles by Dawn Oliver, October 1975 to September 1976. For discussion of the relative pros and cons of using Public Health Act or Housing Act powers see Tom Hadden, *Housing: Repairs and Improvements* (1979), pp. 84-92.)

Local authority powers to require improved plumbing

If a house lacks one of the "standard amenities" for the exclusive use of the occupants, local authorities can require a landlord to instal them, under Part VIII of the Housing Act 1974. The landlord has the right to appeal to the county court against the requirement. Standard amenities are: a fixed bath or shower, a wash handbasin and a sink, all with hot- and cold-water supply and a w.c. If the property is improved in this way, however, the landlord is entitled to apply for an increase in the rent.

In an ordinary house the local authority can only act if asked to do so by the tenant in writing. In tenement buildings the local authority can move of its own motion. A tenement building for this purpose simply means any building containing two or more self-contained flats.

In housing action areas and general improvement areas the local authority can itself initiate action in regard also to private dwellings.

If the work is done voluntarily by the landlord, he can claim half the cost from the local authority. If he defaults after being required to do so, the local authority can do it itself and then recover the *whole cost* from the landlord.

10. *EVICTION*[3]

If the landlord wishes to remove his tenant he may try to persuade him to leave by agreement — sometimes even by offering him sums of money to do so. Any such offer should be viewed with great caution and professional advice on the advisability of accepting should always be obtained. In all probability a landlord who offers money to encourage a tenant to leave is offering less than the true value to him of vacant possession, but only someone with full knowledge of the legal and commercial situation can be expected to advise competently.

Where agreement is not possible, the landlord may consider trying to evict the tenant. If the tenant has an agreement entitling him to stay in the premises for a fixed period he cannot be evicted during the term of the agreement unless he has broken a term or condition and the agreement allows the landlord to forfeit -- which itself however requires a court order. But if, as is more normal, he is just paying rent on a weekly or monthly basis with no fixed period, then whether he can be evicted will depend on whether he can claim the protection of the Rent Acts. But with few

[3] See further especially Andrew Arden and Martin Partington, *Quiet Enjoyment* (Legal Action Group, 1980); Andrew Arden, *Housing: Security and Rent Control* (1978), and Marion Cutting, *A Housing Rights Handbook* (1979).

exceptions, whether protected by the Rent Acts or not, a tenant cannot lawfully be evicted unless he is given written notice to quit and with even fewer exceptions no eviction can lawfully be enforced save after court proceedings which are normally brought in the county court.

Notice to Quit

The circumstances in which a tenant does not need to be given a notice to quit are basically two. One is where he has a fixed term contract. The last day of the tenancy is by definition the end of it and although the tenant often stays on (as a statutory tenant), he does not need to be given a notice to quit. The second main category is that of statutory tenants (for definition see p. 38 above), on the ground that technically the tenancy is deemed already to have been terminated. Otherwise all tenants (whether protected, controlled, shorthold, secure, restricted or unprotected), must be given a notice to quit in writing.

A valid notice to quit means one that requests or orders the removal of the tenant from named premises on a date not less than four weeks hence, ending on a day of the week when rent is due. It must also be at least equal to one full period's length of the tenancy so that a monthly tenancy requires a month's (not four weeks) notice. But only six months' notice is needed to terminate a yearly tenancy. For a notice to quit to be valid, it must contain information about the tenant's rights. It must state that if the tenant does not leave the dwelling, the landlord has to get a court order before the tenant can be lawfully evicted. The notice must specify that the landlord cannot apply for a possession order until the notice to quit has run out.

The notice must also refer to the tenant's rights to obtain legal advice under the Legal Aid Scheme, or from a Citizens' Advice Bureau, a Housing Aid Centre or a rent officer or a rent assessment committee. Failure to state the gist of this information makes the notice to quit invalid. The notice must be served personally on the tenant (or in the case of joint tenants on at least one of them).

Anyone who receives a notice to quit needs advice urgently as to his position but the first assumption should always be that there is no need to act upon it by leaving. It is only the first step in proceedings to have the tenant removed. The next step is court proceedings. No one other than a trespasser can be required to leave without a court hearing.

In most cases it is enough just to wait for the landlord to take the next step by issuing proceedings for possession. However special circumstances affect restricted tenants whose tenancies came into existence before August 1980. They can still get up to six months security provided an application is made to the rent assessment committee (acting for this purpose as the rent tribunal) before the notice to quit expires. The application should ask for a reasonable rent to be fixed and for security of tenure. It is vital to move rapidly since the power to make such an order for security of tenure only exists if the application is made whilst the notice to quit is running.

This does not apply to restricted tenancies that came into effect after the commencement of the Housing Act 1980 since the power to give security of tenure for them lies only in the county court (up to a maximum of three months) and the tenant can therefore simply wait until he is taken to the county court.

A licensee does not have to be given a formal notice to quit but he is entitled to notice which must be reasonable. What constitutes a reasonable period of notice to terminate a licence will depend on all the circumstances. In some cases the licence will be for a fixed period in which case it comes to an end on that date without any notice. A licensee is therefore entitled to a reasonable period of notice or the notice explicitly or implicity agreed between the parties.

Court Proceedings

Under the Protection from Eviction Act 1977 it is unlawful to enforce the eviction of any tenant without going to court. This applies to protected, secure, shorthold, restricted and unprotected tenancies. It makes no difference whether the tenancy is for a fixed term or is periodic. Even licensees and trespassers are normally evicted only after court proceedings, though there is a special speedy procedure available for such cases. A person who receives a summons to appear in the county court on a possession hearing should immediately seek legal advice as to whether there is any valid defence to the proceedings. The main question for decision is whether the tenant should be legally represented for the purpose of arguing his case. This will depend primarily on whether there is a case that can be made. There is little point in spending money to defend a hopeless position. By the same token, however, it is clearly not wise to allow a perfectly sound case to be lost simply for lack of someone to put it to the court. The Court of Appeal has ruled that a tenant who applies for legal aid to help him with the possession summons is entitled to have the case adjourned until the legal aid application has been determined.

Even if it is thought that there is no need for a lawyer actually to argue the tenant's case, there may still be need for someone to prepare the argument for him to present. Legal or other competent advice is therefore vital.

If the tenant loses, he will be ordered to pay the landlord's costs, unless he is legally aided, in which case he will only have to pay a reasonable amount towards his opponents' costs. If he wins, he will get most of his costs paid by the landlord. The judge has power to postpone the order granting the landlord possession, but he will not normally postpone it by more than a few weeks unless the action is for the recovery of unpaid rent. In such cases the court will normally have to order the unpaid rent to be paid off by instalments and will suspend the eviction order providing the instalments are duly paid, together with the current rent. In the case of protected and secure tenancies the possession order cannot be suspended for more than three months. In other cases suspension is limited to two weeks - unless that would cause exceptional hardship for the tenant in which case the stay can be for up to six weeks.

The special procedure for the eviction of licensees and trespassers under Order 26 in the county court or Order 113 in the High Court permits even quicker eviction than under the ordinary processes (see p. 75 below).

Grounds for Eviction

The grounds that have to be established to obtain a lawful eviction vary depending on the nature of the tenancy.

(i) *Tenancy for a fixed period which is still running*

The only ground of eviction during the period fixed in the agreement is if the tenant has failed in some important way to comply with one of the conditions of the lease — such as the agreement to pay rent, or the clause prohibiting subletting without consent. But whether forfeiture of the lease is ordered depends on whether there is a right to forfeit in the lease or agreement and on the discretion of the court.

If the tenancy is a protected or secure one, the landlord will also have to satisfy the court that one of the grounds for eviction exists which apply to such tenancies (see pp. 69-72 below).

(ii) *Tenancy (whether furnished or unfurnished) for a fixed period which has expired*

Unless the landlord has created a new tenancy by accepting rent at the end of a fixed term (which the courts do not easily assume), the previous tenant's rights depend on whether he is protected, secure, restricted or unprotected. If protected or secure, grounds for eviction would have to be shown. If restricted, the court can give the former tenant security for up to three months, unless the tenancy predated the 1980 Act in which case the position is the same as for unprotected tenancies. If the tenancy is unprotected, there is no right in the premises and the court will order that he leave. But the landlord cannot simply put the previous tenant out on the street. He must ask for a court order, though as has been seen, no notice to quit need be served.

(iii) *Regulated tenancies*

In order for a court to order the eviction of a tenant holding a regulated tenancy it must be satisfied of *one* at least of the following possible grounds:

(1) That the landlord can provide suitable alternative

accommodation which is of similar size, rent, convenience and other attributes to that presently occupied.[4]

(2) That the tenant is in arrears with rent payments and that an instalment order for the arrears is not feasible.[6]

(3) That the tenant has broken a condition of the tenancy - but the court will not order eviction unless the breach of condition seems serious.[6]

(4) That the tenant or his family have been a nuisance to the adjoining occupiers.[5]

(5) That the tenant has been convicted of using the premises for immoral or illegal purposes.[5]

(6) That the tenant has damaged the property.[5]

(7) That the tenant has sub-let without consent without keeping any part of the premises for his own use.[6]

(8) That the tenant is overcharging a lawful sub-tenant.[6]

(9) That the tenant was given the premises as an employee, that he is no longer an employee and that the premises are now needed for another employee.[6]

(10) That the landlord needs the property for himself or a member of his family and would suffer more hardship from being deprived of the place than the tenant would in being removed from it. Tenants living at the premises when the landlord first buys it cannot normally be removed on this ground.[7]

(11) That the tenant has damaged the landlord's furniture.[8]

To make an order under any of the preceding grounds the judge must *also* be satisfied that eviction would be reasonable in all the circumstances - which is usually difficult to establish.

In addition there are other grounds which do not require a showing that it would be reasonable to make an order of possession:

(12) That a closing or demolition order has been made for the house or the premises are statutorily overcrowded.

(13) That the tenant was originally served with a notice stating that the premises were the landlord's home and the landlord now wants it back as a residence for himself or any family member who was living there with him when he let it.

[4] See *LAG Bulletin*, December 1976, pp. 280-283
[5] See *LAG Bulletin*, August 1978, pp. 186-189
[6] See *LAG Bulletin*, January 1979, p. 11
[7] See *LAG Bulletin*, January 1978, pp. 10-13
[8] See *LAG Bulletin*, August 1978, pp. 186-189

(14) That the landlord originally gave the tenant notice that he wanted to retire to the home and now needs the premises for his retirement.

(15) The landlord has died and the home is now needed as a residence for a family member living with him at his death or by a successor in title or to dispose of the property with vacant possession.

(16) The property is subject to a mortgage and the mortgagee has acquired the power of sale and requires possession in order to sell with vacant possession.

(17) The home is no longer suited to the needs of the owner having regard to his place of work and he requires it for the purpose of selling with vacant possession in order to use the proceeds to buy a home more suitable to his needs. This ground is designed for someone who lets his home whilst he is sent abroad by his firm and when he returns is sent to some other part of the country.

There are also a number of other miscellaneous grounds for possession. One is where the landlord is a serviceman who at the outset gave the tenant notice that he might want the premises back for his own occupation and he now does. (This only applies however to tenancies that started after 1980.) In such a case the court must make a possession order. Another ground, but one where the court has a discretion, is where the lease is for a fixed period of under eight months and during the previous year the premises were occupied for a holiday let. This is to enable landladies and others with holiday accommodation to let their premises in out-of-season months and get their tenants to leave. There is a similar ground for gaining possession for out-of-season lettings of student lodgings.

It is important to bear in mind that these various grounds of eviction are all very technical. Anyone faced with the eviction (or considering evicting a tenant) should certainly receive competent professional advice as to whether eviction is permitted at law and, if so, how it must be done.

(iv) *Secure tenants*

Secure tenants, most of whom are council tenants, can only lawfully be evicted by an order of the county court. The grounds for regaining possession of a secure tenancy are similar to those for regulated tenancies. Several are identical - rent arrears and other tenancy breaches; nuisance, annoyance, illegality and immorality; causing damage or depreciation of the property; and damage to furniture. In each case the landlord must not only establish the ground but also that it is reasonable in all the circumstances for him to be given possession. There are in addition two further grounds subject to the same test of reasonableness. One is that the tenant induced the landlord to grant the tenancy with a false statement made knowingly or recklessly. Secondly, that the tenancy was granted whilst works were done on other premises of which the tenant, or his predecessor, was a secure tenant and the other premises are once again ready for occupation.

There are three grounds for which the landlord of secure accommodation has to establish simply that suitable alternative accommodation will be available. One is where the occupier is guilty of the offence of causing overcrowding. A second ground is where the landlord wants the premises to carry out work of demolition or reconstruction. The third is where the landlord is a charity and the tenants occupation would conflict with the objects of the charity.

There are also cases where the landlord must show both that it is reasonable for him to have possession and that suitable alternative accommodation is available. One is where the dwelling is adapted for use by the disabled or someone else with special needs and is needed for that purpose. This ground is aimed at the successor of a disabled person or of someone in some other way in need of special facilities. Another is where the dwelling is larger than the tenant reasonably requires and the tenant inherited the premises through succession on death. But this cannot be used against the former tenant's spouse. Also notice of the proceedings must be brought not less than six months nor more than twelve months from the previous tenant's death. The last category in which the landlord must show both reasonableness and the availability of suitable alternative accommodation is when a housing association needs the premises for occupation by someone whose circumstances (other than financial position) make it difficult to find accommodation.

When a secure tenancy comes to an end through expiry of a fixed term or by action for forfeiture when the statutory grounds of possession cannot be shown, a periodic tenancy follows automatically.

(v) *Shorthold tenants*

The court *must* grant a landlord possession against a short-hold tenancy whose tenancy has expired providing there has been no further grant of a tenancy or, if there was such a grant, it was to someone who was originally a shorthold tenant who has been holding on after the shorthold as a protected or statutory tenant.

The landlord must give valid notice to the tenant and must start his proceedings within three months after the notice has expired.

(vi) *Restricted tenancies*

Restricted tenants whose tenancies came into being before August 1980 as has been seen (p. 39 above) should apply immediately to the rent assessment committee (acting as the rent tribunal) for security of tenure for up to six months. Failure to do so before the expiry of the notice to quit results in the rent tribunal not having jurisdiction to grant any security. The result is that the county court can make an order for possession.

Restricted tenancies that came into being after August 1980 are subject to the jurisdiction of the county court which can suspend a possession order for a maximum of three months on such terms as it thinks fit. It must however grant the landlord rent arrears and payment of current rent unless to do so would create exceptional hardship for the tenant or be otherwise unreasonable.

Special Cases

(i) *Deserted wives*

A deserted wife regardless of the nature of the form of occupation, cannot be evicted by her spouse save by an order of the court, which would rarely be made. Under the Matrimonial Homes Act 1967, a wife who is barred from the rented matrimonial home or who is threatened with eviction can go to the High Court or the county court for protection. The court will then make such order as it thinks fit, normally to protect the wife. This is so even if the tenancy is in the name of the husband. (For the position of the deserted wife where the home is owned, not rented, see pp. 85-86. For the position of battered wives see pp. 93-95. For the position of spouses on break up of the marriage see pp. 88-89.)

A deserted wife who is a council tenant can normally retain the tenancy if she keeps up the rent. But if she does not pay the rent, the council may eventually seek to terminate the tenancy. If she wishes to have the tenancy transferred into her name the council may first want her to obtain an order for judicial separation or a divorce. A court can order the transfer of a council tenancy as part of the general financial settlement that follows a divorce.

(ii) *Sub-tenants*

If the landlord is successful in getting his tenant evicted, the position of the sub-tenant depends on whether he was there lawfully or not. If the landlord knew about the sub-tenant and did not object, or positively or tacitly accepted him and if the sub-tenant was therefore a protected or statutory tenant under the Rent Acts, the sub-tenant is protected even if the tenant (his immediate landlord) is evicted. The grounds for possession are the same as for any other protected tenant, see p. 69 above. If however, the sub-letting was not explicitly or implicitly approved by the landlord, the sub-tenant will have to go, though he too is entitled to the normal four weeks' notice to quit. (See *LAG Bulletin*, March 1976, p. 62). In the case of a shorthold tenancy the sub-tenant has no protection even if the sub-tenancy is lawful. So where the landlord becomes entitled to possession against the tenant he can also get possession from the sub-tenant.

(iii) *Where the premises are overcrowded or insanitary*

The protection of the Rent Acts does not apply to unfurnished premises that are overcrowded nor to insanitary premises declared unfit for human habitation. But eviction must, as always, be ordered by a court to be enforceable. In exceptional circumstances the local authority can actually license overcrowding. But unless it has been licensed, the landlord will be able to evict tenants to whom he has himself granted tenancies where the result is to cause overcrowding. Overcrowding is determined by reference to a statutory definition: if two or more persons of opposite sexes over 10 years old (apart from husband and wife) have to share a bedroom, they are overcrowded. Secondly there are a minimum number of rooms (including kitchen and bathroom) per person. Thirdly, the rooms must not be too small. The details of these rules can be obtained from the local Public Health Department.

A tenant living in overcrowded conditions faces not only the possibility of eviction but also of criminal proceedings brought by the local authority — for causing or permitting overcrowding. In practice, however, this does not often occur because the result of the proceedings, if they are successful, is usually the eviction of the family, thus creating a new housing problem for the local authority. The council is now under a legal duty to rehouse someone evicted through overcrowding under the provisions of the Housing (Homeless Persons) Act 1977. There is also a duty under the Land Compensation Act 1973 to rehouse tenants displaced by closing or demolition orders. If the local authority can be persuaded to declare the house in question unfit or to make a closing or demolition order, then the tenants would have the legal right to be rehoused. (See further, p. 78 below.)

(iv) *Squatters*

There are two different ways for evicting squatters. The first is through the use of the civil law - an application for possession from a county court or High Court. Until a few years ago this was procedurally difficult since the owner of the premises would normally be unable to name those he was trying to remove. But under new rules it is no longer necessary to identify the persons affected by the court order. The only requirement is to serve the squatters with a copy of the summons. The court can make an immediate possession order five days later. But even after the issue of the possession order the squatters may still have a little grace. The owner still has to get a writ of possession (in the High Court) or a warrant of possession (in the county court) to enable the under-sheriff (in the High Court) or the bailiff (in the county court) to enforce the possession order. The courts have no power to grant extra time but the under-sheriff or bailiff may take some time actually to enforce the order.

The second approach is through use of the criminal law. Under the Criminal Law Act 1977 anyone who is on premises as a trespasser after having entered as such commits an offence if he fails to leave after being asked to do so on behalf of a displaced residential occupier. It is also a criminal offence to use or threaten violence for the purpose of securing entry on premises providing there is someone there at the time to the knowledge of the person using the violence. "Violence" includes force against property. The displaced occupier of residential premises wishing to recover his own premises (in which he was living immediately before the squatter entered) can use reasonable force to regain entry but in other situations even the owner cannot use force to regain his own premises if the squatters are there. However if the squatters are not there he can use force to enter and remove their belongings.

Alternatively, a displaced residential occupier can ask the police to assist him. If the squatters are asked to leave by the displaced occupier or the police on his behalf and refuse to do so the police have the right to enter and make arrests. The maximum penalty is up to six months imprisonment and/or a fine of up to £1,000.

(v) *When the tenant dies*

A protected tenancy under the Rent Acts can be passed twice on death from the tenant to his spouse living in the premises with him, or if he left no spouse to a member of his family living with him at the time of his death. The new tenant then has exactly the same protection as the old. But on the death of the second new tenant, the tenancy ends. If the landlord then accepts rent from someone living in the house, a new regulated tenancy is created. It will be seen (p. 83) that this right of succession was extended in 1975 to a common law wife with whom the deceased was living for a substantial period - in that case some 21 years. More recently still, in July 1980 the Court of Appeal went even further and held that a married man could succeed his mistress with whom he had been living for nearly 20 years even though they both retained their separate names. (*Watson* v. *Lucas*). But a friend of the opposite sex who lived with the tenant for 20 years in a platonic relationship cannot be a member of the family for this purpose (*Joram Development Ltd.* v. *Sharratt*, 1978).

In the case of secure tenancies the right of succession through death applies only once. The right of succession to secure tenancies accrues to the tenant's spouse or in the case of a joint tenancy, the surviving tenant, or if neither exist, a member of the tenant's family who resided with him during the 12 months before his death.

Illegal Eviction and Harassment

If a tenant leaves of his own accord after having been asked to do so, no offence is committed provided that the landlord has not exerted any improper pressure. But anything beyond a notice to quit could be harassment, which is a criminal offence. The offence consists of doing acts calculated to interfere with the peace or comfort of the residential occupier or members of his household with intent to cause him to give up occupation or to refrain from exercising any right or pursuing any remedy in respect of the premises.

Improper pressure on a tenant to leave includes doing things which have the effect of making it intolerable for him to stay - such as cutting off basic services, or by causing unreasonable noise. Actual eviction by forcibly removing his effects or by changing the locks whilst he is out is clearly illegal.

The police rarely act in harassment cases unless actual violence is involved. In practice therefore the offence of harassment, whether it led to actual eviction or only the threat of eviction, is dealt with normally in the magistrates' court on complaint brought by the housing department of the local authority. Penalties have however usually been derisory. Failing this the tenant can bring a private prosecution at his own expense. The magistrates, since the Criminal Justice Act 1972, also have the power to order the defendant to pay the victim damages. But if they decline to do so, or if the prosecution does not, for one or another reason succeed, the only way in which the tenant can get any remedy which directly benefits him is by bringing a civil action in the county court - for an injunction and damages. The injunction orders the landlord to desist from his hostile acts and, if the tenant has been evicted, to restore him to possession. The damages are compensation for the wrong done by the landlord. Until 1977 a request for an injunction had to be combined with a claim for damages but it is now possible to ask for an injunction on its own.

The Court of Appeal ruled in 1975 that harassment under section 30 of the Rent Act 1965 (now s. 1 of the Protection from Eviction Act 1977) did not give rise to an action in the civil courts but only to criminal proceedings. An action for damages and an injunction in a civil court must, therefore, be based on some other ground - such as breach of the covenant for quiet enjoyment, breach of contract, trespass, intimidation, or assault.

If the tenant has been actually evicted, speed is vital. If the application for an injunction is delayed even a week it may fail simply because, by that time, the tenant will probably have found alternative accommodation. But if he is still living in a hotel, hostel or other temporary place the judge may be willing to order that he be returned to his home - providing that this has not in the meanwhile been let to some other person who moved in without knowing anything about the fate of his predecessor.

Damages for wrongful eviction can be as high as several hundred pounds. (In one very bad case in 1977 the county court awarded £1,000 and the Court of Appeal upheld the decision - *LAG Bulletin*, December 1977, p. 287.) The claim can include reimbursement for hotel or other bills, taxis, removal vans and other incidentals as well as the inconvenience, insult and worry caused by the illegal eviction. It may be possible to get aggravated or exemplary damages.

Any adviser aware of the plight of someone threatened by improper pressure with eviction or who has been forcibly evicted without a court order should arrange for the victim to have legal advice without delay. Sometimes the mere threat of immediate legal action for an injunction and damages, together with mention of the possibility of criminal proceedings, is enough to secure reinstatement. Legal aid is available for civil actions but not to help a tenant bring a private prosecution. (See *LAG Bulletin*, April 1975, p. 104; and generally Andrew Arden and Martin Partington, *Quiet Enjoyment*, LAG, 1980.)

11. *THE COUNCIL'S DUTY TO REHOUSE*

In most circumstances local authorities have no legal duty to house anyone. Local authorities have a wide discretion which can rarely be challenged in the courts. There are, however, some situations where there is a legal right to be rehoused.

Thus the council has obligations to rehouse on *slum clearance*. A council must satisfy itself before declaring a slum-clearance area that it can rehouse those displaced. Before taking action on the slum clearance the authority has to undertake to carry out its rehousing obligations within a period regarded as reasonable by the Minister. In practice, this duty is to some extent reduced in effectiveness by the fact that slum-clearance plans normally take years to carry out and by the time they are implemented many of the local residents who would be entitled to be rehoused have moved elsewhere.

Apart from slum clearance, where anyone is displaced from residential accommodation by the council's acquisition of land through a compulsory purchase order he has a right to be rehoused (Land Compensation Act 1973, s. 39). Those who qualify are those resident when the order is first published. This means a few days after the order is signed and sealed but shortly before the first notification to residents which follows on the council's resolution to make the order.

A right to be rehoused also arises under section 39 of the Land Compensation Act 1973 where the council have made *a housing order* and no suitable accommodation is available. A housing order includes a demolition or closing order. Those who qualify are those resident in the affected building on the date when the order was made.

The duty does not apply to trespassers but it does apply to lodgers and lawful sub-tenants. The Court of Appeal has held, however, that the duty under section 39 can be temporarily satisfied by the provision of temporary accommodation: (*Hendy* v. *Bristol Corporation, The Times*, November 2, 1973).

The third main situation where there is in some sense a rehousing obligation is for those who are *homeless*. The duty to house the homeless arises under the Housing (Homeless Persons) Act 1977. This creates an enforceable duty to provide accommodation to a person who is homeless or is threatened with homelessness provided: he has a priority need; that he did not become homeless intentionally; and that he has some connection with the area to which he applies or, if not, that he does not have a local connection with another area. The Act states that a local authority must have regard to the Department of the Environment's Code of

Guidance. A "priority need" means one of the following: dependent children living with the applicant; homelessness arising out of an emergency such as fire, flood or other disaster; the applicant or someone reasonably living with him is vulnerable through old age, mental illness, physical disability or other special reason; or pregnancy.

"Intentional homelessness" is deliberately doing something or failing to do something which results in not occupying accommodation which it would have been reasonable to go on occupying. An act or omission is not deliberate if it was done (or omitted) in "good faith on the part of a person who was unaware of any relevant fact."

A person has a "local connection" with another area through having been normally resident there or being employed there or through family assocations or because of "any special circumstances."

A person is "homeless" if he has no place that he has the right to occupy together with those who normally live with him or he has been locked out of his home or continued occupation would lead to violence or a real threat of violence. A person is "threatened with homelessness" if it is likely that he will become homeless within 28 days.

The courts have ruled that the Act can be enforced not merely by an order to house someone but also by an action for damages.

The duty of the local authority is not simply to house someone qualified who is already homeless, but to provide appropriate assistance for those who are homeless but are not qualified (for instance because they do not have a priority need or became homeless intentionally). There is a duty to provide *temporary* accommodation for those who are homeless intentionally. There is also a measure of protection for those threatened with homelessness. (For a general guide to the Act see A. Arden, *LAG Bulletin*, November 1977; for cases on the Act see especially *LAG Bulletin*, January 1980, p. 14; for details of the standard of accommodation that should be provided for homeless persons see D. Ormandy, *LAG Bulletin*, December 1977, p. 288.)

The extent of the duty under the Act may be judged from the case of Mrs. Alan Streeting, an Ethiopian woman who came to this country from abroad after going through a form of marriage ceremy with Mr. Streeting, not knowing that he was already married. They lived together abroad and he cared for her child though it was not his. Later he died and she came here. The Home Office gave her refugee status in November 1979 and she applied to the Hillingdon council for assistance under the Act. The council admitted that she was homeless, that she had a priority need because of her dependent child and that she had not become homeless intentionally. But it denied that they owed her any duty since she had no local connection with any housing authority in Great Britain. The Court of Appeal held that this did not matter. A person who had been allowed into this country by the immigration authorities and who had not become homeless intentionally could claim the right of assistance under the Act even though he or she had no local connection.

5 The Family

1. *THE LEGAL PROS AND CONS OF GETTING MARRIED*[1]

A couple who are living together may need advice as to whether there are significant advantages from a legal point of view in their getting married. Whether the differences between the married or unmarried state are advantages or otherwise, will usually depend on whether the advice is sought by the man or the woman.

● The man's duty to support the woman he lives with, for instance, applies only if she is his wife. But if they have children, the father has a duty to maintain them whether or not he is married to their mother.

● Custody of legitimate children is granted by the courts to whichever parent is best for the child. The basic right to custody of an illegitimate child is in the mother. The father of an illegitimate child has no *right* to custody but he can apply to the court for an order for custody or access under the Guardianship of Minors Act 1971.

● Unmarried parents cannot jointly adopt their own child.

● Illegitimate children have the same right to inherit from a parent as those who are legitimate. But they do not have any right to inherit property from other relatives unless left something in a will.

● Many social security benefits available to wives cannot be claimed by the common-law wife. These include widow's allowances, widowed mother's allowance, widow's pension and maternity benefit on the man's insurance. She can, however, seek supplementary benefit for herself and her children if deserted. Whilst cohabiting they are treated as man and wife for the purposes of supplementary benefit. An

[1] See further M. Parry, *Cohabitation Social Work and Law* (1981)

unmarried couple with one or more children can get family income supplement but only the man can claim it.

●A wife has a right to inherit her husband's estate unless he makes a will and deprives her of her inheritance. The cohabitee has no such right. But both a wife and a cohabitee can apply to the court on the ground that the deceased failed to make "reasonable financial provision" for her (see p. 144 below).

●A common-law wife normally has no legally protected right to remain in a home owned or rented by her man, however long they have been living there together. One exception is where she has contributed money or work to the purchase of the home. (But helping to buy the house by simply lending money to the purchaser does not normally create a right to share the property - apart of course from the right to have the money repaid.) Another way of gaining a share in the property itself is where he has given her a share in it — for instance, by putting the house into joint names or by expressing an intention to give a share in the house to her. If the property is protected by the Rent Acts (see pp. 37-38 above), a common-law wife can be protected from eviction after the death of her man especially if there are young children living in the household. In those circumstances, the law gives her the same rights as a widow to stay on as the lawful tenant after the death of the tenant.

But unmarried partners are slowly gaining better protection at law. In a 1975 Court of Appeal decision (*Dyson Holdings* v. *Fox*), for instance, an unmarried woman who had lived for some 21 years (without children) with a tenant protected under the Rent Acts was said to be a member of his "family" for the purpose of the rule that members of the family may succeed the statutory tenant on his death (see p. 76 above). The Domestic Violence and Matrimonial Proceedings Act 1976 gave a cohabitee the right to apply for an injunction to restrain her partner from molesting the applicant or a child or to exclude him from the home or a part of it (even though it may be his own home) or to permit the applicant to enter the home. It is not necessary to prove violence. Such an injunction is seen by the courts as a temporary measure pending other arrangements being made. It is not designed to transfer property rights to the cohabitee. A three month period is quite typical. (On the position of the cohabitee in the home generally see *LAG Bulletin*, December 1978, p. 288).

2. THE LEGAL POSITION OF MAN AND WIFE WHEN THE MARRIAGE IS A GOING CONCERN

The legal relations between man and wife rarely have much importance until the marriage starts to go wrong. No one, for instance, is much interested as to who in law owns what or who can decide what until there is serious disagreement between the couple. It is usually assumed that the problems will be solved through the ordinary processes of give and take or discussion rather than according to strict legal rules. Occasionally, however, it is helpful to know what the legal position is, if only as a basis for deciding that the law does not provide the best basis for solving the issue. Application can always be made to the court under section 17 of the Married Women's Property Act 1882 to get a ruling as to who owns what. This applies both during the marriage and after it has ended, though an application by a former spouse must be brought within three years of decree absolute.

Money

A wife has no legal right to know what her husband is earning nor to receive any particular proportion of his pay cheque. She does have a basic legal right to be maintained financially by him and this is enforceable in the courts (see pp. 89-91 below). An order for the payment of maintenance can be obtained and enforced even whilst spouses are cohabiting though if the order is made by the magistrates it is not enforceable after they have lived together for a continuous period of six months.

The Matrimonial Home

Each party to a marriage has the duty to cohabit with the other. This means that even a husband who owns his house cannot in law bar his wife's entry to the house, for she has a legal duty to live with him and he has a legal duty to allow her to live with him, as well as a legal duty to live with her. If he attempts to keep her out, she can go to the Family Division of the High Court or the county court for an order that he admit her. If there is any fear that the husband-owner will try to put her out or even to sell or mortgage the house without her consent, she should immediately ask a solicitor to register her right to occupy the house at the Land Registry or the Land Charges Registry. This can be done without any great expense and, once done, protects the non-owning spouse from the danger of losing her home through a sale by her husband.

Precisely the same principles apply to the situation of the wife whose husband is the tenant. Registration will prevent the husband from transferring the tenancy to someone else. Nor can she be evicted by her husband the tenant, since this would put him in desertion and would be prevented by the courts. This is true whether she is in a furnished, unfurnished or council tenancy.

Where the property is "registered land" a wife who has contributed money or money's worth toward the purchase of the house would be protected even if no charge is registered. This is the effect of a decision of the House of Lords in June 1980 (*Williams and Glyn's Bank* v. *Boland and Brown*). The judges held that a wife who had contributed her money toward the purchase but was not mentioned on the title deeds could not be required to leave by the bank to which her husband had morgaged the house. The bank was deemed to have notice of her interest in the house simply because of her "actual occupation." The rule would apply not only to wives but to anyone who had an interest in the property - cohabitees, friends or anyone who had contributed to the purchase price and was in occupation.

Obviously, if the wife or cohabitee is the part-owner of the property or co-tenant, her rights to occupation would be even stronger. She does not need the protection of the registration of a charge, for, being part-owner, she cannot be required to leave without her consent or an order of the court.

Other Assets

Property that each owned prior to the marriage continues to be the property of that spouse. Property acquired after the marriage usually belongs to the spouses in the proportion that they contribute to its price. So, if the husband buys the furniture for the matrimonial home out of his own earnings it belongs to him. This usually penalises the wife, especially if she is not working. Her only, extremely limited, protection derives from the rule that property purchased out of an allowance paid by husband to wife for family expenses belongs to each equally. Also, if there is a joint bank account, unless the arrangement is clearly otherwise, the law presumes that each owns half, even though only the husband pays into it. The presumption is that he makes a gift of half to her.

Sex in Marriage

Refusal or inability to consummate a marriage by sexual intercourse are grounds for annulment of the marriage.

Unreasonable refusal of sexual intercourse could constitute grounds for the other party to ask for divorce (on the grounds of unreasonable behaviour); so, too, at the opposite extreme, could excess of sexual demands.

Suing each Other

There is nothing in law to prevent one spouse from suing the other and in one common situation this can in fact be a very valuable right. Where one spouse is injured whilst a passenger in a car driven negligently by the other, the injured person can sue the other. All drivers are now required to be insured for injuries to passengers and the insurance company will therefore have to pay the damages. An action need create no antagonism or disagreeable repercussions for the spouses and there is therefore no reason why they should not be advised to pursue such a claim. The only contra-indication would be in the case of very minor injuries when the damages obtainable might be outweighed in value by the no claims bonus which would be lost.

3. *FINANCIAL SUPPORT OF CHILDREN*

The father of a child has a legal duty to provide financial support for him, whether or not he is legitimate. If he fails to provide this support, the mother can go to the magistrates' court for an order that weekly payments be made or for a lump sum of up to £500.

A woman wishing to apply for maintenace for her

illegitimate child should go to her local magistrates' court and ask for a summons to be served on the alleged father. The mother will have to prove that he *was* the father. This can be done by producing any witness who can say, or any document, including a letter, which shows or suggests that he is the father of the child. The court can order a blood test with the agreement of the subject but this will only be conclusive negatively. A blood test can never prove that A is the child of B. It may, however, prove conclusively that he is not.

The application to the court must be made within three years of the birth of the child unless the father paid money for the maintenance of the child before the birth or within the three year period. Living with the mother and contributing to household expenses could count as contributing to the maintenance of the child.

If the child is legitimate, application can be made to the High Court, the county court or the magistrates' court. In the magistrates' court, however, an order can now be enforced even if the parties to the marriage continue to cohabit but not if cohabitation goes on beyond six months. In the High Court and the county court this condition does not apply.

An order in favour of a child whether legitimate or not normally lasts until the age of 18 but it can go on longer if the child is in full-time education, or there are special circumstances.

Help with Costs of Schooling

Free school meals are available to children in families getting supplementary benefit, family income supplement or who are in special need because of low income. In the last category the parents will have to apply to the education officer with evidence of their income. The social worker may be able to assist in preparing the case.

Local education authorities have discretionary powers to make grants towards the cost of school uniform.

4. UPBRINGING OF CHILDREN

Prior to 1973, the law gave the father a dominant right in relation to decisions about the upbringing of the children. If the parents disagree on such questions as schooling or religious upbringing, the father's view would in law be regarded as decisive. But the Guardianship Act 1973 specifically provides that both spouses have an equal right to determine questions regarding the upbringing of their children - as well as any question regarding the disposition or use of any property or income held in trust for minor children. In the event of a dispute the Act provides that either spouse may take the issue to court (the Family Division of the High Court, the county court or the magistrates' court). The court then has an absolute discretion to decide whatever it thinks is in the best interests of the child.

5. *THE LEGAL POSITION WHEN A MARRIAGE IS BREAKING DOWN*

When a marriage starts to break down the main legal problems, pending a decision one way or the other on the marriage, are eviction, financial support and custody of children and formalities of separation.

(a) *Eviction*

Under the Matrimonial Homes Act 1967 the owner or tenant cannot turn his (or her) spouse out of the matrimonial home. An application can be made to the High Court or to the county court but the court has a complete discretion as to whether the non-owner spouse should be asked to leave the home. The conduct of the parties is one of the crucial questions which will influence the court's decision. Normally it is most unlikely that the court would order the removal of the wife, especially if there are minor children.

As has been seen, the danger of the non-owner or non-tenant spouse being evicted by a third person to whom the premises are sold, mortgaged or transferred is eliminated by first registering an interest as a land charge. But where one spouse, (normally the wife) has no legal title to the home or tenancy although she cannot be evicted it is also true that she cannot normally, before a divorce, get an order requiring the other spouse to leave.

Where both spouses share the legal title to the home, neither can evict the other without an order of the court. The court would normally only permit this on a sale of the home and then only if it was not unjust to the objecting party. Where a house is being or has been bought, a spouse can acquire legal title by having his or her name on the title deeds or by making financial contributions to the cost of the home or of improvements. Under the Domestic Violence and Matrimonial Proceedings Act 1976 the court has power to order a spouse who is owner of the home or tenancy to leave. If one spouse is maltreating the other, the victim could instead ask the court for an order of non-molestation. Breach of such an order could lead to commital for contempt of court. The courts have power to regulate the exercise of the right to occupy the home and this could involve an order allocating different parts of the home to the parties.

As will be seen below (p. 94) there is now also a new power to ask a magistrates' court for an order to exclude a violent spouse from the matrimonial home.

(b) *Financial Support*

A wife whose marriage is breaking down and whose husband is not supporting her adequately can go to the magistrates' courts, or to the county court or to the High Court for an order of financial support. Maintenance can be ordered in respect of both the wife and the children of the family. A child is "of the family" if it has been treated as one whether or not it has been acknowledged as such and regardless of knowledge of true paternity. Orders can require payment direct to the child. This may in some circumstances have tax advantages. Otherwise in the normal case payments are made to the court and then are paid out to the wife, normally now through the post. If the husband fails to pay, the wife can ask the court to order that payments be deducted from his wages. Further failure to pay can ultimately be penalised by imprisonment.

A wife who is not being maintained by her husband or who has children who are not being maintained can in addition ask for supplementary benefit. The advantage of this is that it is a reliable source of income as compared with the fluctuating income from an erring husband.

When a wife applies for supplementary benefit because her husband is failing in his duty to maintain her and/or the children, the Supplementary Benefits office may try to get her to take out maintenance proceedings in the magistrates' courts though this is no longer official policy. It is important to appreciate that the wife cannot be forced to take such proceedings if, for any reason, she does not want to and, if she refuses, her right to supplementary benefit will not be affected. If she is unwilling, the Supplementary Benefit authorities are entitled to take either civil or criminal proceedings against the husband. In fact, it is often preferable to go to the county court rather than the magistrates' court for maintenance. The county court does not have the association with criminal cases of the magistrates' courts. The county court has full power to make orders for a lump sum payment as well as periodical instalments and such orders can be secured. The magistrates now have power to make lump sum orders under the 1978 Domestic Proceedings and Magistrates' Courts Act but the lump sum order cannot be for an amount greater than £500. Also orders by magistrates for periodical payments cannot be secured. The grounds for making an order of maintenance in the magistrates' courts are slightly different from those in the divorce courts. The 1978 Act contemplates such orders where the respondent has failed to provide reasonable maintenance for the spouse or any child of the family, or where he has behaved in such a way that it is not reasonable to expect the spouse to live with him or where the applicant has been deserted. Adultery is no longer a bar to maintenance ordered by magistrates but the court is permitted to have regard to the conduct of the spouses so far as this is relevant. There is also power to make an order where the parties agree and where they have been living apart by agreement for not less than three months and the respondent has been making periodical payments to the applicant.

Previously, an order made by magistrates could not be enforced if the parties were still cohabiting. This has been modified by the 1978 Act, so that it now only applies if they have been living together for more than six continuous months. (Even then an order can still be enforced insofar as it is payable to a child of the family.) The six months rule however does not apply in the county courts. In both the county court and in the magistrates' court it is possible to get an interim order. In both too an order ceases on remarriage. The rules are now also the same as to the period of an order for a child. In the first place orders are limited to the birthday following the upper age for compulsory schooling (16), "unless the court thinks it right in the circumstances to make a longer order." But the order can go on if the child is in full-time education.

In any event, a wife ought always to take legal advice before deciding whether and, if so, where to take proceedings for maintenance. If she is not being regularly maintained by her husband she will normally be eligible for free legal advice from a solicitor on the green form scheme (p. 15 above).

If the wife has a maintenace order from the court which is being paid irregularly, the wife is in the unhappy situation of not knowing each week whether or not she will get her money and whether, therefore, she will have the basis of a claim for supplementary benefit to make up her payment to her full entitlement. The way round this is to instruct the court to pay any money received under the maintenance order to the Department of Health and Social Security. (The court is not obliged to agree to this, but most do.) The Supplementary Benefits office can then issue an order book at the full rate of supplementary benefit entitlement without regard to what, if any, money comes in from the husband. A Home Office circular (8/74) said the procedure ought to operate wherever the woman signs an authority for such diversion of payments.

For wives wishing to claim maintenance from husbands overseas there are various procedures, depending on the country the husband is living in. (See *LAG Bulletin* August 1975, p. 206 and August 1976, p. 179.)

(c) *Custody of Children*

The same court that makes an order for maintenance can also decide the question of custody of children. The basic principle is that the court gives custody to whichever parent is best for the child. The interests of the child are paramount. Normally the courts take the view that the mother should have the custody of very small children, but even this basic principle is not invariable. The conduct of the parents towards each other is not regarded as crucial, save in so far as it reflects on the question of the best interests of the child. But there is no longer any feeling that an adulterous wife necessarily forfeits her right to the children. Unless altered, the order continues until the age of 18.

Where the children are old enough, the court will ask them

for their opinion. The views of experts such as child psychiatrists, social workers or court welfare officers will be taken into account. So too will the amount of disruption that would be involved if the children were moved. Other things being equal, the court is likely to order that the children stay with whichever parent is remaining in the matrimonial home.

The parent who loses custody will normally be permitted access; the order will probably stipulate reasonable access, leaving the parties to make their own arrangements. If the court separates "custody" from "care and control" this means that the spouse with "custody" is supposed to take the principal decisions about the upbringing of the child but the other spouse has the day to day management. Such orders are not common. In case of dispute the parties can go back to the court for clarification of the order. (Under the Domestic Proceedings and Magistrate's Courts Act 1978 there is now also a right for grandparents to ask for access. Such requests can be made whether the child is legitimate or not.)

Applications for custody should be made sooner rather than later. There is no need for the marriage to have finally broken down. Nor is there necessarily any need for the party making the application already to have found accommodation. Obviously it is preferable, but it is not a firm rule that custody can only be awarded to a party who has definite accommodation. This is important in practice since local authorities and housing associations sometimes refuse to give a woman a tenancy until they know whether or not she will have children with her.

If there is any danger of one parent "snatching" the children and departing, especially abroad, the other parent should take immediate legal advice. The county court or the Family Division of the High Court can be asked for an injunction at very short notice. An emergency legal aid certificate can be obtained even over the telephone in cases of real urgency. Making a child a ward of court is perhaps the most effective technique, since the mere issue of the summons makes it unlawful to remove the child from the jurisdiction. The court then issues a letter which tells the Home Office that the child is a ward of court and should not be allowed out of the country. If there is no High Court Registry in the vicinity, the next most convenient course is to issue a Guardianship of Minors Act summons in the local county court and obtain an injunction prohibiting removal.

Where a custody order is made by a court (including a

magistrates' court) it has the power to direct that no one may take the child out of the jurisdiction without the consent of the court. A written notice lodged in the passport office prevents the issue of a passport without this consent.

(d) *Protection for the Battered Wife (or Cohabitee)*

A wife who is being physically assaulted by her husband can seek protection at law. There are two main approaches - the civil and the criminal.

In the criminal sphere the main remedy is a summons for assault in the magistrates' court. The wife would go to the local magistrates' court and swear an information on the basis of which the court is asked to issue a summons. The penalties available to the court range from binding the defendant over, to putting him in prison for a maximum of six months.

Legal aid is not available to the wife for this type of case since in criminal cases legal aid is only given to the defendant. On the other hand, if the wife can handle the case without legal representation, the costs will be slight. If she needs help, she may be able to get it from a social worker or other lay adviser or from some form of legal advice centre.

The criminal law in this sphere is not however very useful. Much more powerful remedies exist through use of civil remedies - to obtain an injunction and an order to exclude the violent spouse from the home.

There are three main sources for such remedies. One is the right of the High Court and the county court to issue an injunction in connection with pending matrimonial proceedings for divorce or judicial separation. Frequently however no such proceedings have been started and more urgent steps are required. In this situation a swift remedy exists through the 1976 Domestic Violence and Matrimonial Proceedings Act in the High Court or county court, or, alternatively, through the 1978 Domestic Proceedings and Magistrates' Courts Act in the magistrates' courts.

The 1976 Act permits a non-molestation injunction for the wife and any children living with her even if they are not children of the family. The court can also make an order excluding the man from the home or from part of it even if he owns it - though only for a period. If she has left the home with the children the court can order that she be allowed back and that he leave. The 1976 Act applies not only as between married partners, but also to cohabitees. (For a guide to the procedure to be followed see Peter Johnson, *LAG Bulletin*, August 1977, p. 185.)

The 1978 Act permits the magistrates to make a personal protection and/or an exclusion order. A personal protection order can be granted if the man has either threatened or committed violence against the woman or a child of the family. (The 1978 Act does not protect a foster child or other child who is not a "child of the family"). An exclusion order requiring the man to leave the home and not to return can be granted on proof that he has committed violence against the applicant or a child of the family or that he has threatened violence against them and has actually committed it against someone else. The magistrates must also be satisfied that the applicant or a child is in danger of being "physically injured" by the man. The 1978 Act only applies as between spouses and does not therefore assist a cohabitee.

Both injunctions in the county courts and personal protection orders can be obtained as a matter of urgency and in the absence even of the other party (*i.e. ex parte*). Emergency injunctions can be obtained from the judge out of office hours; an emergency application for an expedited personal protection order from magistrates must be made during court hours. But no expedited exclusion order can be obtained. (For guidance as to the procedure see J. Levin, *LAG Bulletin*, December 1979, p. 286).

Both the 1976 and the 1978 Acts give the court the power to order attach an order for the arrest of the man if he breaks the injunction - with the result that he is then brought back before the court. Enforcement of injunctions is through proceedings for contempt with imprisonment as the ultimate sanction. Magistrates have no power to commit for contempt of court. Instead they can order the defendant to pay up to £50 per day for every day in breach of the order or a sum of not more than £1,000. But there is also a power to order the imprisonment of the respondent for up to two months until he complies with the order.

A battered wife should certainly be helped to obtain competent legal advice. In 1975 the National Women's Aid Federation was formed. Its address is 374 Gray's Inn Road, London WC1 (01-837 9316). Welsh Women's Aid is at 2 Coburn Street, Cardiff (Cardiff 3888291). Scottish Women's Aid is at Ainslie House, 11 St. Colme Street, Edinburgh EH3 6AA (031-8011 or 229-2798 and 041-429 5759). There are now some 150 women's aid centres in towns and cities throughout the country. See also generally *Battered Women and the New Law* by Anna Coote and Tess Gill, published jointly by Inter-Action and the National Council for Civil Liberties (1979), 85p.

(e) *Formalities of Separation*

Many marriages drift apart with no formal steps taken to bring them to an end. The only way finally to end a marriage is to secure a divorce or annulment but there are lesser forms of termination of the marriage.

One is a simple, private separation agreement or exchange of letters usually providing for payment of a certain amount of maintenance and for the arrangements regarding the children. The trouble with this kind of very informal agreement is that it may not be treated as legally binding by the court and may therefore be difficult to get it enforced.

Slightly more formal is the *separation or maintenance deed* drawn up by lawyers. The danger of this is that, if there is any reason to fear that either party will oppose a divorce, the deed should not actually refer to an agreement to separate. If the deed states that the parties have agreed to separate, both are subsequently precluded from bringing divorce proceedings on the ground of desertion. (It does not, however, prevent such proceedings on other grounds). If the parties are likely to agree to divorce, there is no equivalent problem since divorce by consent is now permitted after two years' living apart.

A third form of separation arrangement is a decree of judicial separation from a divorce court. Such decrees are not common - less than a thousand are made in a year. They are used to obtain orders for maintenance and custody over children where neither party wishes to get a divorce but wishes to regularise the fact of separation. The effect of a decree is to end the duty to live together. A decree of judicial separation acts in the same way as a decree of divorce for the purposes of intestate succession. Neither spouse can succeed to the estate of the other save by the terms of a will.

To obtain a decree of judicial separation it is sufficient to be able to establish any of the facts on which a divorce can be granted: that the other party has committed adultery, or behaved unreasonably, or has deserted the petitioner for five years or that they have lived apart by agreement for two or more years or they have lived apart for five years.

A decree does not order the parties to live separately. It is not therefore an adequate way of protecting a wife from a violent husband.

6. *ENDING THE MARRIAGE*

There are two ways to end a marriage - annulment and divorce.

(a) *Annulment*

In certain rare cases marriages are dissolved on the grounds that they have never legally existed. This occurs when one or other spouse was under the age of 16 at the time of the marriage; where the marriage was bigamous; or where the parties were within the prohibited degrees of family relationship.

In certain other, almost equally rare, cases the marriage is dissolved on the grounds that it was vitiated by some defect. A marriage undertaken as a result of physical duress could be terminated on the ground that there was never any genuine consent to the ceremony. Failure to consummate the marriage is grounds for annulment - whatever the cause of the failure. It is also grounds for annulment that at the time of marriage one of the parties was suffering from VD or that the wife was pregnant by another man or that at the time of marriage either party was suffering from mental illness which made him or her unfit for married life. (This last ground only applies to marriages celebrated after July 1971.)

A petition for a nullity decree is made to a divorce court. If undefended, this means the county court; if defended, it means the High Court. The assistance of a solicitor will normally be advisable and legal aid will normally be obtainable.

(b) *Divorce*

The overwhelming majority of marriages that end other than through death end in divorce.

There is today only one main test of whether the court can grant a divorce - has the marriage irretrievably broken down.

The old concept that in order to obtain a divorce one had to be able to prove that the other party had committed a matrimonial offence has been abolished. But the old matrimonial offences in fact live on since they are one of the ways of establishing that the marriage has broken down.

There are today five ways in which breakdown of the marriage can be established:

(1) *Adultery.* The petitioner must show that the other partner has committed adultery and that (whether because of the adultery or for other reasons) it has become intolerable to live with him or her.

Adultery means sexual intercourse; intimate acts short of actual intercourse do not qualify. Proof is usually by circumstantial evidence or confession of one or other or both of the adulterers. Often it is obtained by an inquiry agent acting on the instructions of the other spouse.

Providing the petition is undefended, as most are, proof that marital life has become intolerable is usually not difficult.

(2) *Desertion for two or more years.* Desertion means that one marriage partner has left the other without reasonable excuse. To leave for good reason, for instance, because of the other spouse's unreasonable conduct, is not desertion. Indeed, the wife who feels compelled to leave because of her husband's unreasonable conduct could herself petition for divorce on the ground of desertion.

It is not necessary to show that the parties lived apart continuously for two years, providing they have lived apart for not less than a total of two years in the two and a half years prior to the date of the petition. In other words, up to six months is allowed by law for attempts at reconciliation without penalty if they fail.

If a husband leaves a wife and subsequently wants to return, that may end the desertion. If the wife unreasonably refuses to have him back, she becomes the deserter. But if she is reasonable in refusing to have him back because, for instance, he has previously been violent towards her or their children, the desertion would continue.

A wife who commits adultery while deserted by her husband may lose her right to accuse him of desertion, unless she can show that he either does not know or care.

(3) *Living apart for two or more years.* If both parties agree, they can now obtain a divorce on the ground of breakdown of marriage simply by showing that they have lived apart for a total of two years in the two and a half years prior to the petition. They must, however, have regarded the marriage at an end throughout the two-year period. Separation for two years whilst the husband is abroad for military duty, for instance, would not count unless they treated the marriage as over.

(4) *Living apart for five years.* After five years of separate living, either party can obtain a divorce whether or not the other consents. The only ground on which a divorce can be resisted on this ground is that it would cause grave financial or other hardship - usually to the wife. This could apply, for instance, if a divorce would result in a dutiful wife losing the financial security of her husband's pension. The court may not grant the divorce unless the husband can make some appropriate financial arrangements to protect the wife. But the judge will weigh up the unfairness to the wife against the claim of the husband and of any second family he may have acquired. The conduct of the parties could also be relevant.

(5) *Unreasonable behaviour.* It is no longer necessary to show that the conduct of the other spouse caused physical or mental ill-health. It is enough to show that the conduct is such that it would not be reasonable to expect the petitioner to go on living with the other spouse. Violence, habitual drunkenness or abusive conduct will normally justify a petition, but conduct which is much less obviously serious may also suffice. Even merely feckless conduct may be enough, providing it is so aggravating as to be justification for the other spouse to regard it as intolerable. It is not necessary to show that the conduct complained of was intended. So insanity, which is no longer a separate ground for divorce, would normally constitute sufficient reason for divorce on the ground of unreasonable conduct.

How quickly can a divorce be obtained?

A divorce cannot normally be obtained until the parties have been married for at least three years. The only exception is where exceptional hardship can be shown, for instance, in the form of danger to life, limb or mental stability.

Cost of a divorce

The cost of a divorce depends on whether one represents oneself or has legal aid or has to pay solicitors. Under new rules the procedures for getting the actual divorce have now been so streamlined that no hearing for the actual divorce is normally required providing the petition is undefended. (If there are minor children there will be a hearing so that the judge can express himself satisfied with the arrangements made for them.) Most divorces are now handled by this procedure under which the decree nisi is pronounced by the judge in his chambers simply on inspection of the papers with neither the parties nor any lawyers present! The decree absolute is given in open court but the parties need not be there.

A person who does his own undefended divorce has to pay a filing fee of £35, but anyone on supplementary benefit or family income supplement is exempt from this fee. Divorce forms are free of charge. There are various books designed to assist the layman conduct his own divorce and the Lord Chancellor's Office has published a booklet entitled "Undefended Divorce" available from county courts free of charge. But most clients of social workers will not necessarily feel able to handle even this relativlely simple procedure without legal advice.

Those eligible for help under the green form scheme (p. 15 above) can get a lawyer to fill out the forms and help generally.[2] If there is a dispute about children and/or property it is also possible to obtain full legal aid. But full legal aid is no longer available to get a divorce itself - unless the proceedings are contested.

Normally where a person who is legally aided recovers money or property through the legal proceedings he has to pay the legal aid fund for his costs out of the proceeds before getting the remaining balance. However in the case of money or property recovered through matrimonial proceedings the first £2,500 recovered is exempt from the effect of the so-called charge.

[2] In divorce cases the solicitor working under the green form scheme can now do £55 worth of work without prior permission from the legal aid authorities

A person who is not eligible for legal aid who requires the services of lawyers for a divorce will have to pay costs that are unlikely to be less than £100 and could be considerably more. But if the petition is brought against the husband he will normally be ordered to pay the wife's costs.

How long will it take to get a divorce?

Obtaining a divorce will normally take at least six months from start to finish. If the case is defended, the delay will be longer. There is a waiting period of six weeks from the date of the decree nisi to the decree absolute. If any irregularities are discovered in this period the divorce may be cancelled. But the divorce cannot be withheld simply on the ground of adultery in this period.

Children and divorce

If there are minor children, no divorce can be obtained unless the court is satisfied that appropriate arrangements for them have been made. If the parties to the marriage agree, the court normally makes a custody order at the same time as granting the decree nisi. If there is a dispute, the court will delay granting the decree until evidence has been heard in private to enable it to decide the question of custody.

The best interests of the children are the court's prime guide. As has been seen (see p. 91 above), normally a mother will be given small children, irrespective of her conduct. But if, in the particular circumstances, this is not in the best interests of the children, the court will give custody to the father.

The parent who loses custody will normally be permitted reasonable access. Sometimes, the court will separate custody from care and control. One parent will have the day to day management of the children (care and control), whilst the other is given the power to decide major questions such as education and general upbringing (custody). Such orders are, however, rare.

A child who is the subject of a custody order cannot be taken out of the country without the written consent of the other party. If this is refused, the other parent can ask the county court for permission.

Where it is feared that either parent may take the children

out of the country without the consent of the other, a court injunction can be sought and in emergencies obtained at very short notice.

7. *FINANCIAL ARRANGEMENTS FOR WIFE AND CHILDREN*

After a divorce or annulment the court makes such orders as appear appropriate for the maintenace of the wife and children and for the disposition of the family assets. If, as is normal, the case is undefended, the court usually endorses an agreed settlement worked out by the parties or their lawyers.

The court has a complete discretion to order that one spouse pay regular sums and/or transfer savings, capital or other assets such as the home or part of it to the other for the benefit of the other spouse or the children.

The court can take into account all relevant factors - the age of the parties, their respective means, or earning capacity, their obligations to others, the length of the marriage and their conduct.

A wife without children who is divorced after three or four years and is capable of earning her own living might receive no maintenance for herself. The conduct of the parties is today, however, of relatively minor concern. Even a wife who has behaved badly can expect to get her full share of the matrimonial assets - unless her conduct has been so appalling that the court feels she should be penalised.

In one case, for instance, a 40-year-old wife who had had an adulterous affair with a 20-year-old son of friends who lived in the house with the family was held entitled to her full share with no deduction for her conduct.

The courts tend to operate a rough rule of thumb that a wife's maintenance should normally be limited to about one-third of their gross combined income plus one-third of his capital. The matrimonial home is usually made available, by one means or another, to a mother with minor children over whom she is given custody.

The court can make orders irrespective of the ownership of the property. So a husband who owns everything can be ordered to transfer to his wife half the value of the house or two-thirds of his shares, or one-quarter of his savings or what-

ever other assets the judge thinks appropriate. Property for
this purpose has been held to include a council house tenancy.
But the court would not order a council tenancy to be transferred to the wife against the wishes of the council.

Those advising parties to a marriage that is breaking up
should have in mind that there are many financial implications.
Careful and competent advice can make a considerable
difference to the assets available . Thus, the amount of tax
paid may depend on whether maintenance is paid voluntarily
or under a separation agreement or as a result of a court
order. Additional child relief may be available through
separating rather than staying under one roof. A divorce can
add income to the income of a woman over 60 whose
husband is still working, since it will count as the death of
her husband entitling her to a retirement pension, whether or
not she is still in work. Claims for rent and rate rebates will
often be greater where the husband pays the maintenance and
the wife pays rent and rates than where the husband pays for
these direct. Eligibility for supplementary benefit can
increase if maintenance is paid direct to a child rather than to
the mother. There may be a financial advantage in the wife
claiming child tax reliefs rather than the husband. (There is a
valuable article on these problems in the *LAG Bulletin*,
September 1975, p. 240; see also *LAG Bulletin*, July 1976, p.
152; and *LAG Bulletin*, May 1980, p. 119.)

Variation of Orders

Any order for regular weekly or monthly payments can be
varied on application of either party. A wife who knows that
her husband's financial circumstances have greatly improved
can go back to the court to ask that the payments for herself
or the children be increased. Conversely, a husband who loses
his job can ask that the payment be reduced. If a wife in
receipt of maintenance remarries, the husband is entitled to
stop the payments to her but remarriage does not affect payments to the children. The new husband is not required to
take on the financial responsibility for the children of the
former marriage.

On the other hand, where the parties come to a final disposition of their assets which is approved by the court it may
not be possible to have it re-opened. If for instance the wife
accepts the matrimonial home in full settlement of her claims

and the court dismisses her claim for maintenance by consent she may not be allowed later to ask for maintenance for herself. The House of Lords said in 1979 (in *Minton* v. *Minton*) that the law encouraged the parties to make a clean break and to begin a new life which is not overshadowed by the relationship which has broken down. It would be inconsistent with this principle if the court could not make a genuinely final order. But this principle of the "clean break" does not apply to any order made in regard to the maintenance of children. Nor would it affect the right to ask for a variation of the ordinary order for weekly or monthly maintenance payments.

6   Personal Injuries

When a person suffers personal injuries two kinds of financial claims may come into issue - a claim for damages and social security.

1. *CLAIMS FOR DAMAGES*

The first vital principle to have in mind is that many people who are entitled to damages never realise this. Ignorance of one's rights is as common in this area as in many others. In a survey large numbers of cases were discovered of individuals who had been injured and had then thrown away perfectly good (and in some cases valuable) claims for damages simply through ignorance. There are a variety of common misconceptions which prevent people from making legitimate claims:

"It was my fault" - Victims often fail to realise that when they slip, fall, trip or otherwise injure themselves the fault can often be laid wholly, or, at least, partly on someone else - notably on an employer. Employers are under a legal duty to provide a safe system of work and defective steps, floors, machinery, ladders, etc., can often be attributed to a failure by the employer to comply with his legal duties.

"It was mainly my fault" - Victims frequently do not appreciate that, if any part of the blame can be laid at someone else's door, a claim will be valid. Damages are reduced to the extent that the victim was at fault, but this may still leave a substantial and worthwhile amount to be recovered from the other party.

"It was my workmate's fault and I would't want to sue him" - If a workmate was wholly or partly responsible for the

injury, the employer can be sued for vicarious liability. Theoretically, the employer can then turn round and sue his own employee, but in practice this virtually never happens. It is therefore nearly always safe to sue an employer for the negligence of a fellow employee.

"There were no witnesses, so I couldn't prove anything" - The evidence of the victim himself is evidence and can be the basis of a claim, even if there is no one else to corroborate it.

"I wouldn't want to sue my employer; I might get the sack" - It would be an extremely bad employer who would even consider sacking an employee for this reason. The employer is normally insured against the risk of accidents and a claim is therefore within the ordinary course of business. Moreover, so far as employees who have been with the same firm for 52 or more weeks are concerned, such a dismissal would be an unfair dismissal entitling him to damages (see p. 148 below).

"There is no need to claim as I am already drawing my industrial injury (or other social security benefit)" - The fact that one is already drawing or will draw sickness, injury or disablement benefit does not prevent a claim being made. The effect of such payments is that one half of the amount that is likely to be received over five years from the date of the accident has to be deducted from the compensation.

"There is no need to claim as I am getting my wages (or half my wages) whilst off work" - The employee who is getting his full wages off work obviously cannot claim loss of present earnings. (Though if he is receiving less than full wages, he can sue for the balance). But he is entitled to make all the other claims open to an injured person - for pain and suffering, loss of future earnings, loss of amenity and general disability (see pp. 107-108 below).

"I don't need the money as I took out insurance against just such a risk" - Insurance moneys do not have to be deducted in any way from a claim for damages. The law takes the view that the person who has the foresight to take out insurance should not be prevented from making a full claim for someone else's negligence.

"It wouldn't be worth the trouble of claiming" - Whether

something is worthwhile is obviously a subjective question, depending on a whole variety of circumstances. An adviser may, however, be able to persuade an injured person that little bother or trouble is involved in at least taking preliminary professional advice to see whether a claim is open and what, in broad terms, it might be worth. It is also worth noting that even apparently minor injuries can sometimes warrant significant amounts of money. In the survey referred to there were a number of cases in which the victim might have claimed if he had realised the sums to which the injury might have entitled him. In one case a woman was injured when the bus she was on moved away. The bus conductor rang the bell too soon. She suffered bruising and shock and had since developed a hernia which was aggravated by the fall. Her husband said that they had not even tried to get compensation because "I didn't think the expenditure of time and money would be worth it." This claim could have been worth £250. In another case a man's car was in collision with another car as a result of his brakes failing. His wife was injured in the accident and was off work for two months. She would have had a claim against him (payable by his insurers) but no claim was made. The husband said "I didn't want to bother," but the claim could have been worth £200 plus loss of earnings. In another case a man had his finger smashed and was off work for five weeks when a piano he was shifting fell as a result of faulty wheels. He thought it was the fault either of his workmates or of his employer but made no claim because, as he said, "It wasn't worth it. I was financially O.K. at the time." The claim would have been worth at least £100 plus loss of wages. (These were 1967 figures.)

"I couldn't afford to bring a claim, lawyers are too expensive" - A person entitled to take advantage of the legal advice and assistance scheme (p. 15 above) can get advice free or fairly cheaply. If his income or savings put him outside the means test limits there is also the Fixed Fee scheme providing half an hour's diagnostic advice for £5 regardless of means. If the injuries result in a successful claim, the costs of the injured person's lawyers are borne by the other side.

"I wouldn't want the disgrace/trouble/worry of a court case" - The overwhelming majority of personal injury claims are settled through negotiation and never reach court at all.

What has to be proved?

A claim for damages for personal injuries is normally based on an allegation of negligence. In order to establish a claim for negligence it is necessary to establish three things:
1. that the victim was owed a duty of care by the person who caused the injury
2. that the duty of care was broken
3. that injury resulted.
Basically what it comes down to is whether the person who caused or contributed to the injury took reasonable care in all the circumstances.

There are also situations, mainly arising out of injuries at work, in which an employer is liable even if he was as careful as anyone could be, and it is therefore impossible to prove negligence. In such situations, usually of particular danger, the law has provided that liability exists even without proof of fault. It is enough to show that an accident causing injury occurred from such a cause.

A lay adviser, unless he has considerable experience of such matters, should be extremely chary of giving an injured person the feeling that it is not worth discovering whether his injury may entitle him to make a claim. On the contrary, normally he should help him secure competent advice - whether from his trade union, a Citizens' Advice Bureau, a legal advice facility or a solicitor in private practice. Failure to get such advice may cost the injured person dear. It should also be remembered that, if a claim is to be made, it must be brought in time. The time limit on personal injuries actions is normally three years from the date of the accident, though special rules apply if the injury was only discovered later, which occurs especially with certain kinds of industrial diseases. Claims should however be made as early as possible. (See further, p. 172.)

What damages can be claimed?

There are various heads of damages:

● *Actual financial loss.* Lost wages or salary; money laid out as a result of the accident (in repairing clothes, close relatives taking taxis to the hospital, employing someone in the house to help, private medical treatment, if recommended by the doctors, etc.).

● *Probable future financial loss.* Lost wages are calculated for the difference between what the injured person would probably have earned and what he can now be expected to earn after the accident. The courts have fixed 15 years as the normal maximum period for which such damages can be calculated, even for a man in his twenties. For someone older it may be less. Allowance has to be made for income tax and national insurance that would have been paid on wages. Allowance must also be made for non-recoverable sick pay from the employer. Tax refunds and half the amount payable for five years from the date of the accident from the DHSS by way of injury or disablement or sickness benefit also has to be brought into account.

● *Pain, suffering, disability.* The courts award sums for the pain of the injury (including continuing pain), and for any loss of capacity to enjoy life as before - loss of the sense of smell, loss of the ability to go ballroom dancing or to do gardening, loss of one's pleasant temperament, etc. Such awards can sometimes be very large, running into thousands of pounds.

● *Damages for death.* There are two kinds of claim if someone was killed in the accident. One is for *his* injuries - including any pain and suffering and his reduced expectancy of life. The maximum under this (life expectancy) head of damages is usually low - currently not more than £1,250 or so. The second, and normally much more substantial, claim is for the loss of financial support brought by his family. Relatives can sue to the extent that they can show that *they* were financially dependent on the deceased. The claim is for a lump sum calculated on the basis of the deceased's probable earnings (less tax) in the future.

From whom can damages be claimed?

A claim is made against the person legally responsible. In the case of work accidents this usually means the employer; in the case of road accidents it is normally the driver of one's own car or of another car (or both). But unless the person being sued is extremely wealthy (or the claim is a minor one) it would not normally be worth going ahead unless he was insured. Employers and motorists usually carry the relevant forms of insurance so that a claim will be met by the insurance company. Householders often do not carry insurance in regard to injuries in the home, which helps to explain why so few of such accidents results in claims. (Another reason is that often there is no legal duty of care towards the person injured, or the accident is wholly caused by the victim's own carelessness.)

There are, however, two situations in which it is worth claiming even though the person responsible for the injury has no money, is not insured or cannot even be found.

(*a*) If the injury is caused in the course of a criminal attack, it is rarely worth suing the criminal - even assuming he can be identified and found. A claim can however be made to the Criminal Injuries Compensation Board, see p. 126 below. The great advantage from the claimant's point of view is that it is not necessary to do more than to show that the injury occurred as a result of a criminal assault. There is no need to prove that any attempt was made to find or to proceed against the assailant. The Board is very helpful to claimants and there is usually no need to employ lawyers to make the claim. (For a helpful guide to making such claims see *LAG Bulletin*, February 1978, p. 36.)

(*b*) If the injury is caused by a hit-and-run motorist or by a motorist who is not insured, the Motor Insurer's Bureau may pay up. This is an organisation set up by the insurance companies to meet claims by untraced or uninsured drivers. Claims are made to the Bureau at Aldermary House, Queen Street, London EC4. They can cover death or injury resulting from an accident in Great Britain. Application must be made in writing within three years of the accident. Obviously, however, it is best to make a claim sooner rather than later.

Actually making the claim

Negotiating a settlement for a personal injury claim is a test of nerve and judgment. The person with experience will normally do better than one without it. Even amongst professionals, such as solicitors, the practitioner who handles a great volume of personal injury work will tend to recover

more for his client than the one who only has occasional
cases of this kind.

The basic rule of thumb is that a settlement offered in the
early stages is likely to be for an amount below what the
claim is worth and should probably be refused. A person
injured in an accident who is called upon by a representative
of the person or company concerned and offered something
in full settlement of the claim should be told that, if an offer
is made from the outset, it may be worth a good deal more
than the amount first mentioned.

The second rule of thumb is that unless injury is manifestly
trivial, professional advice should be brought in before any
settlement is concluded.

2. *SOCIAL SECURITY*

For anyone who loses money through being off work, social
security provides three main forms of assistance - sickness
benefit, industrial injury benefit and disablement benefit.
These are dealt with in the next chapter.

7 Social Security

Social security is a subject of great practical importance for social workers' clients. Mastery of the subject can make an immense difference in terms of actual cash in the client's pocket. It is notorious that take-up of welfare benefits is a problem. Many fail to get their entitlement due to ignorance and a social worker who is knowledgeable and concerned in this field may be able to make a considerable impact. (Treatment of the subject here is inevitably brief. For fuller details see in particular Child Poverty Action Group, *National Welfare Benefits Handbook**; Ruth Lister, *Welfare Benefits* (Sweet & Maxwell, 1981); Harry Calvert, *Social Security Law* (Sweet & Maxwell, 2nd ed., 1980); and Ogus and Barendt, *The Law of Social Security* (Butterworths, 1978). There are also a large number of Department of Health and Social Security (DHSS) leaflets. These are usually obtainable from local offices but in case of difficulty they can be obtained from DHSS Leaflets Unit, P.O. Box 21, Stanmore, Middlesex HA7 1AY.

1. *INTRODUCTION*

There are two main types of benefit - those that are means-tested and those that are not. The theory behind means-tested benefits is that scarce resources should be restricted to circumstances where the individual can demonstrate that he needs the cash. Inevitably this system is costly since it requires detailed examination of the financial position of the individual claimant. It is also liable to create in the mind of the individual a sense of humiliation in subjecting himself to the indignity of a scrutiny of his affairs. This in turn may affect the take-up rate. The chief means-tested benefits are supplementary benefit, family income supplement, and rent and rate rebates.

*See also CPAG, Mark Rowland, *Rights Guide to non-means tested Social Security Benefits* (CPAG).

Benefits that are not means-tested are based on the assumption that in certain types of situations individuals will require extra assistance and the extent of the assistance is generalised so that broadly everyone gets the same benefit regardless of means (though the better off find part of the benefit "clawed back" through taxation). The main benefits in this category are national insurance (covering, for instance, unemployment, sickness, invalidity, maternity, retirement and old age benefits), industrial injuries and disablement benefit and child benefit.

Some non-means tested benefits are flat-rate, others are earnings-related reflecting differentials in wages. In many instances the flat-rate system is supplemented by an earnings-related additional payment. Flat-rate benefits include invalidity benefit, attendance allowance, mobility grant, maternity grant, child benefit and death grant. Benefits that have an earnings-related element include unemployment and sickness benefit, retirement pensions, widow's allowance and industrial injury benefit. Benefits whether flat-rate or earnings-related frequently adjust to the size of families through additional payment for dependants.

Some types of benefit are based on the contribution principle - the claimant in order to qualify must show that he or some other relevant person such as a husband has contributed over a period of time to the national scheme. Benefits that depend on contributions include unemployment benefit, invalidity and sickness benefit, retirement pensions, widow's benefit, death grant and maternity benefits. Those that are not based on any contributory element include child benefit, supplementary benefit, family income supplement, attendance, invalid care and mobility allowances, old age pensions, widow's pension and guardian's allowance.

Rates of benefit normally change in November and contribution rates change in April. All the latest rates for the time being are set out in leaflet NI. 196 which it is useful to have. The Leaflet Unit send this or any other leaflet on a regular basis free of charge.

Types of benefit

The DHSS leaflet *Which Benefit?* lists 60 different ways to get cash help from the state in times of need. The account that follows deals with the chief types. The treatment is brief - only supplementary benefit receives detailed discussion since this is one benefit above all where the intervention and assistance of a social worker can make a difference.

2. *SUPPLEMENTARY BENEFIT*

Supplementary benefits affect close to five million people. The great majority of these receive supplementary benefit in addition to national insurance or industrial benefits. The system tops up payments for pensioners, widows, the unemployed, sick or disabled. There are also close to a million other persons who do not qualify for national insurance benefits, but who get supplementary benefit as unmarried mothers, separated wives, unemployed men, single women looking after elderly relatives and others.

The supplementary benefit system has recently been significantly affected by legislative changes. Thus the Social Security Act 1980 and the Regulations made under that Act have introduced alterations in the system affecting in particular the way in which income and needs are assessed. The 1980 Act abolished the Supplementary Benefits Commission, and replaced it with an Advisory Committee. Decisions on matters of policy will now be taken by the Secretary of State rather than by the independent Commission.

But the chief change is that the 1980 Regulations prescribe in great detail how income and needs are to be assessed. Formerly much of the information about these decisions was contained in the secret "A" code which was available to officers who operated the system but was unavailable to claimants and their advisers. Secondly, whereas the previous system and the "A" Code left the officers great discretion, the new regulations are much more precise. The discretion was designed to enable payments to be tailor-made for the needs of the claimant but the vast increase in the numbers being handled, the complexity of the system and the inevitable differences of approach from office to office meant that the system became overloaded and inequitable through a lack of uniformity in application. The objective now being pursued is therefore drastically to reduce the scope for discretion. The Secretary of State Mr. Patrick Jenkin in introducing the regulations to the House of Commons on July 28, 1980 said:

"The main change that we are making in this first stage

of the reform is to convert discretion into entitlement. Instead of there being a wide measure of discretion exercised by officers of my Department under the guidance of the Supplementary Benefits Commission, there will be legal rules clearly set out in regulations with published guidance to help claimants and their advisers. Claimants will be entitled to a written statement of their benefit. There will be a new adjudication system, similar to the national insurance scheme with a final right of appeal to the Social Security Commissioner.''

The Minister also said that his Department would issue free explanatory leaflets that would be available from local DHSS offices and a new revised edition of the Supplementary Benefits Handbook which is sold by H.M. Stationery Office and is used in particular by those who have to advise claimants. Reference should be made to them for guidance, since the Regulations themselves are extremely difficult to comprehend unless one is a considerable expert in the field. It is also clear that the Regulations still leave a good deal of room for argument and discretion. Since the claimant now gets not only a statement of his benefit but of how it is calculated, the explanatory leaflets and the Handbook (plus any detailed books or pamphlets) should be of real value in checking whether he or she has been given the right amount.*

Those entitled to supplementary benefit: Claimants must be over 16 and living in this country. It is not necessary to be a citizen. Aliens and immigrants who are resident here can apply but visitors and overseas students would not normally be entitled save for emergency situations. For those who receive benefit who are over pension age it is called supplementary pension; for those who are under pension age it is called supplementary allowance.

Those not entitled: Certain categories are not entitled to claim benefit. The most important is that of persons in full-time work. If such persons have dependent children they may however be entitled to family income supplement (see p. 120

---

*See also *LAG Bulletin*, November 1980, p. 259 and December 1980, p. 285; *New Law Journal*, January 15, 1981, p. 71 and following issues.

below). A claimant who is unemployed but whose wife is in full-time work is not disqualified. The second main exclusion is that of young people still at school or receiving full-time education. Such children are included as dependants in their parents' assessment.

The requirement to register for work: Most applicants are required to register for work but this does not apply to a man over 65 or a woman over 60 nor to the sick or disabled, nor to those solely responsible for looking after children under 16. A person who has to look after a sick relative may be excused the requirement to register for work.

The claimant's household: The resources and requirements of husband and wife are added and so too are those of children at home in full-time education. But the resources of other members of the household are not taken into account.

When an unmarried couple are living together as man and wife they are treated as a married couple. This so-called cohabitation rule has given rise to much difficulty and complaint.[1] In a special report on the subject in 1976 the Supplementary Benefit Commission said that the criteria for determining whether a couple are living together depends on close analysis of the facts of the relationship. The elements that are especially relevant were said to be:

(a) Are they members of the same household? This implies that the man "normally lives under the same roof" and "usually, that he has no other home where he normally lives." It implies he lives there regularly apart from visits to relatives or absences due to work, etc. This is said to be an indispensable factor.

(b) Is the relationship more than an occasional or brief one? There must be some (but it is not clear how much) duration to it. The Commission will not assume that a new relationship constitutes "living together" until it has been continuing at least for some weeks.

(c) The fact that a man is "bearing a major share of the household expenses, as distinct from paying rent or for board and lodging" will normally be taken as evidence that they are

[1] On the cohabitation rule see, especially, the Commission's *Handbook* and their 1976 Paper, *Living Together as Husband and Wife*; the Commission's Report, *Cohabitation: the administration of the relevant provisions of the Ministry of Social Security Act 1966*, (1971); and Ruth Lister, *As Man and Wife*, CPAG Poverty Research Series No. 2.

living together. But it will not in itself be conclusive. Even
without financial support they could still be found to be
living together.

(d) A sexual relationship or the absence of one is not in
itself conclusive, but it could be significant. If a couple are
living together in circumstances where a sexual relationship
seems likely to exist it is not necessary to *prove* that it
actually does exist. But if there was no reason to suppose
that a sexual relationship did exist it would be unlikely that
a man and woman would be said to be living together.

(e) Where the claimant is caring for children of the union
there will be a strong presumption that she and the man
should be regarded as living together as husband and wife.
But evidence that he did not act as father to the children
might be "very carefully considered."

Generally, "What has to be decided is whether the relationship, as a whole, of a couple living together in the same
household has the character of that of a husband and wife."
Where a claimant for supplementary benefit disputes that she
is cohabiting she will be given a leaflet explaining the
official interpretation of the law. If and when benefit
is withdrawn she will get a written decision together with a
copy of her own statement and details of any additional
information on which the decision was based.

Each case must be judged on its merits and facts. SB officers
and investigators use whatever methods seem appropriate to
ferret out the fact, including the use of neighbourly gossip,
snooping and clandestine surveillance.

Assessment of income: Basically all income is counted in
assessing resources. This includes social security payments
such as child benefit and national insurance benefits. It also
includes maintenance payments whether paid under a court
order or not. The income of dependent children however is
not counted. There are also other disregards. From November
1980 one is a standard £4 in respect of the income of anyone
whose income is taken into account. If both husband and
wife are earning something the total disregard is therefore £8.
In the case of single parent families, in addition to the basic
disregard of £4, a further amount equal to one half of income
of between £4 and £20 can be ignored. This gives a single
parent a maximum disregard of £12 per week.

Assessment of capital: From November 1980 the assessment of capital has been greatly simplified. The value of an owner occupied house and personal possessions is ignored. So too is the first £2,000 of savings. But savings of more than £2,000 make the claimant ineligible.

Assessment of benefit:

(a) *Normal requirements.* The benefit paid is the difference between the claimant's actual income and the relevant scale figure. The scale rates are higher for those who have been on supplementary benefit for one year (previously two years), and for invalids and one-parent families. Pensioners get the higher rate immediately. There is also an addition to the standard scale rates for people who are blind. The scale rate depends on whether one is single or married and on the age of dependent children. (From November 1980 there are only three categories of dependent children instead of five as before: 0-10, 11-15 and 16-17.) The basic scale rate is supposed to cover all normal requirements which is defined in the regulations as meaning "all items of normal expenditure on day-to-day living . . . including in particular food, household fuel, the purchase, cleaning, repair and replacement of clothing and footwear, normal travel costs, weekly laundry costs, miscellaneous household expenses such as toilet articles, cleaning materials, window cleaning and the replacement of small household goods (for example crockery, cutlery, cooking utensils, light bulbs) and leisure and amenity items such as television licence and rental, newspapers, confectionary and tobacco." The figure for normal requirements does not however cover the cost of housing.

In regard to housing costs the regulations provide that the net amount paid in respect of rent and mortgage interest shall be added to the basic scale rates, subject to certain adjustments and exceptions. Thus a fixed amount is deducted for lighting and heating if these are included in the rent - because heating and lighting are already included in the basic scale rate. The proceeds from sub-letting similarly have to be deducted. Normally supplementary benefit pays the whole of the rent or mortgage outgoings but a senior officer has the power to refuse to pay the whole amount where the claimant is found to be occupying excessively large or luxurious accommodation or where it is situated in an especially expensive neighbourhood. A claimant who has an earning son or daughter or other non-dependant living in the household has the weekly housing addition reduced by a flat-rate for every such person (£4.60 as at November 1980).

(b) *Adjustment for exceptional circumstances of a continuing character.* An extra sum is added on for special circumstances. Thus there is an extra heating allowance (in November 1980 of £1.40, £2.80 or £3.40 depending on the situation) to those who need extra heating because of, say, old age, ill-health or dampness in the home; an extra allowance for persons needing special diet, or who have to be given a bath or need other attendance, or who have to do laundry away from the home because the adults in the home are too old or ill or there are no suitable facilities.

(c) *Special circumstances not of a continuing character: single payments.* Prior to 1980 the Commission had a power to award a single payment of benefit to meet exceptional need where it appeared reasonable to do so. This broad discretion was capable of covering a great variety of needs. One of the chief objectives of the 1980 change in the system was considerably to restrict this discretion. (See *Guidance to Supplementary Benefit Offices: Claims for single payments*, DHSS, 85p). There remains a power to make single payments for exceptional circumstances but a separate set of regulations is intended to make the system more uniform and predetermined. One change is that single exceptional payments can normally be made to someone already in receipt of regular supplementary benefit - though the power to make payments to anyone on ground of urgent need for instance after a disaster such as fire or flood remains. (Repayment of such grants to meet urgent needs may be requested).

The regulations state that no single payments can be made for a variety of listed purposes - such as travel expenses to and from school, school uniform or sports equipment, costs of motor vehicles, installation, rental or call charges of telephones, holidays, TV or radio. Single payments *can* be made to meet, for instance, maternity expenses, funeral expenses of a close relative (as defined), draughtproofing, the installation of a fuel meter, the cost of essential repairs needed to preserve a house in habitable condition up to a limit of £225, etc. But in each case the regulations state with considerable particularity the exact circumstances which qualify

- there is little room for "interpretation." So maternity payments for instance are intended to cover such things as clothes, nappies, feeding bottles, a cot with mattress, pram and baby bath but it is prescribed that in the case of the last three items they should be second-hand! (Legitimate funeral expenses cover the cost of a "plain coffin," transport for the coffin plus one additional car, and the reasonable cost of flowers). Grants cannot be made to meet normal wear and tear or a need which has arisen in the normal course of events for instance because a child has outgrown clothes. Needs that could be met are clothes for a pregnant woman, for someone who has lost or gained weight, for heavy wear and tear caused by disability, for clothing accidentally lost, damaged or destroyed, or for clothing needed because of an illness or disability.

If a special need is not actually mentioned in the regulations the only hope is Regulation 30 which gives the supplementary benefit authorities the power to make a discretionary payment. This power only exists however where in the opinion of the officer such a payment is the only means by which serious damage or serious risk to the health or safety of any member of the family can be prevented. This is intended to be an extremely narrow general discretion.

Note

For the poor with children it is also worth bearing in mind that the local social services department may be able to help with benefits in cash or kind under the authority of section 1 of the Child Care Act 1980 (formerly s. 1 of the Children and Young Persons Act 1963). This provides that "it shall be the duty of every local authority to make available such advice, guidance and assistance as promote the welfare of children . . . [including] provision for giving assistance in kind or, in exceptional circumstances, in cash."

The duty under section 1 overlaps with the area covered by Supplementary Benefit. Yet there are many local authorities which take advantage of their powers to make money and other help available to the poor. But there are great differences between local authorities. Typical payments are for such things as gas, electricity, or central heating bills or rent arrears, as well as items in kind such as cookers, mattresses or general household equipment.

Although the Act specifies that money payments are exceptional, there are some authorities where they are quite common.

3. *FAMILY INCOME SUPPLEMENT (FIS)*

FIS was introduced in 1970 to meet the needs of low-paid families with one or more dependent children. At least one child must be living with the family and be under 16 or if more than 16 then still at school. Entitlement is limited to those in full-time work, which for couples means that the man is working at least 30 hours a week and for one parent families work of not less than 24 hours a week. (A couple for this purpose need not be married providing they are living together as man and wife).

The total family income must be below the qualifying level. The rates change regularly but in November 1980 the qualifying level for those with one child was an income of under £67 a week. For each extra child one could earn an extra £7 a week and still qualify.

To arrive at "family income" one adds all money coming in including all earnings before deductions from full and part-time work by both partners but excluding: child benefit, attendance or mobility allowance, the first £4 of war pension, rent allowance, any income of the children and any payment received for children boarded out with the family.

The amount received is fixed - there is no discretion to adjust it according to need. Again it varies depending on the size of the family. The formula is that one receives half the difference between total family income and the qualifying level for a person with that number of children, subject however to an overall maximum. So a person with two dependent children in 1980 had a qualifying level of £81. If the family income was £61 the FIS payment would be half of the difference of £20, or £10. But the maximum in 1980 was £17 plus £1.50 for each child additional to the first.

Claims have to be in writing on the prescribed form (FIS 1) and must be sent to the DHSS in Blackpool from where the scheme is administered. Once the claim is allowed payments normally continue for a year even if circumstances change for the better or worse in that period.

Anyone entitled to FIS is also automatically entitled to

certain other benefits such as free school meals, free milk and vitamins, free NHS dental treatment, glasses and prescriptions (see leaflet M. 11).

4. *RENT AND RATES*

As has been seen (pp. 53-55 above) those with inadequate incomes can apply to the local council for rent rebates (for council tenants), rent allowances (private tenants) or rate rebates (council tenants, private tenants and owner occupiers). The amount of the rebate or allowance depends on income. For further information get the relevant leaflet from the local council or a Citizens' Advice Bureau. (*There's Money Off Rent* and *How To Pay Less Rates*).

5. *EXPECTING AND HAVING A BABY*

There are two national insurance maternity benefits: maternity grant and maternity allowance.

Almost all mothers can get a *maternity grant*. This is a single lump sum intended to help with the expenses of having a baby. It is payable on either the husband's or the wife's national insurance contributions (but contributions paid at the reduced rate for married women or widows do not count). A claim can be made from the fourteenth week before the baby is due to three months after it was born. (The claim is valid even if the baby is still-born provided the pregnancy lasted at least 28 weeks). If twins or triplets are born the payment is made for each child.

Further details are given in Leaflet N1.17A. Claims are made by filling in Form BM 4 from a social security office or maternity clinic.

Maternity allowance is paid only on the mother's national insurance contribution. A woman who has paid full contribution can apply for a weekly fixed sum for up to 18 weeks plus an earnings related supplement and a further sum for any dependent child. (The earnings related supplement is to be abolished in 1982). The sums payable are not taxable. Payments start in the eleventh week before the baby is due. Claims should therefore be made as soon as possible after the fourteenth week before the birth. If the claim is made late payments may be lost. If the claim is made after the birth it is limited to payments for the week of the confinement and the following six weeks. The allowance is only payable for days on which no paid work is done. Maternity pay from the employer does not disentitle one but paid work does.

For details of the contribution conditions and other details see Leaflet N1.17A. Claims are made on Form BM.4.

A woman who stops work on having a baby may also have a right to six weeks *paid maternity leave* from her employer. This statutory right applies to a person who has worked for the same employer for two or more years eleven weeks before the baby is due. The money, which is taxable, is paid by the employer who can claim it back from the Department of Employment. The rate is nine-tenths of normal weekly pay less the flat-rate maternity allowance -whether or not one is getting it. In order to get paid maternity leave one must give the employer three weeks' written notice. (See further Leaflet PL.625 from the unemployment benefit office.)

6. *CHILDREN*

Child benefit is a flat-rate, non-taxable amount payable in respect of every child under 16 (or under 19 and still in full-time education). The benefit is paid to a parent or other person responsible for the child - normally the person with whom the child is living. Claims are made on form CH2 obtainable from a social security office. Lone parents (whether divorced, separated or single) may be entitled to an extra small amount known as Child Benefit increase - see Leaflet CH.1.

Guardian's allowance is a weekly tax free sum paid to a person who takes an orphan child into the family and gets child benefit for that child. Claims are made on form BG.1. (For further information see Leaflet N1.14).

Child's special allowance is payable to a divorced woman with a child if her former husband dies providing she has not remarried. It only applies however if the husband was liable to pay some maintenance to support the child. (See Leaflet N1.93.)

Allowances or benefits associated with school are available for low income families. These include free school meals, free school milk, fares to school, school uniform and clothing grants all of which are available through the Education Office or the Education Welfare Office of the local authority.

7. *UNEMPLOYMENT*

A person who is out of work and who has paid Class 1 (employee's) national insurance contributions can claim *unemployment benefit* providing he is fit and available for work. The benefit provides a basic rate plus further sums for a wife and dependants. There is also an earnings related supplement but this is to be abolished in 1982. (See Leaflet N1.12 and N1.155A). Unemployment benefit is payable for up to one year and the earnings related supplement for up to six months.

Another form of payment arising out of unemployment is for *redundancy* (see pp. 150-151 below).

8. *ILLNESS*

People who are normally employed or self-employed but who cannot work because of sickness can claim *sickness benefit*. There is a basic rate and an earnings related supplement. (The earnings related supplement is to be abolished in 1982). There are also increases for a wife and one other adult dependant and for each dependent child. Payments are not taxable.

Payments depend on meeting the conditions for Class 1 or Class 2 contributions but those who do not fully meet these conditions may be able to get reduced rates. The conditions and other details are set out in Leaflet N1.16.

Sickness benefit is payable for up to 28 weeks. After that the claimant who is still off work will have to claim invalidity benefit instead.

Invalidity pension is available where a person has been off work for a total of 168 days - either continuously or in broken periods providing the break is no more than 13 weeks. The benefit goes on until one returns to work or age 65 (for men) or 60 (women) whichever is earlier. Payments are not taxable. (See generally Leaflet N1.16A).

Those who do not qualify through failure to satisfy the contribution conditions may still get a non-contributory invalidity pension. (See Leaflet N1.210 for men and single women and Leaflet N1.214 for married women).

Hospital travel expenses can be claimed by low income out-patients and in-patients (for admission and discharge). Those on supplementary benefit or FIS qualify automatically but others can also apply. Those on supplementary benefit or FIS apply by taking their order book to the hospital. People with low income use the claim form in Leaflet H.11.

When a person who is receiving social security benefits goes into hospital the local social security office should be informed. This is because some benefits are reduced or stopped during a hospital stay. The office should also be told of the discharge date. (See Leaflet N1.9).

9. *INJURIES AT WORK*

Employees who cannot work because of an accident at work or some industrial diseases are entitled to *industrial injury benefit*. The benefit does not depend on contributions. It provides a basic rate for up to six months from the date of the accident and increases for a wife and adult dependants and for dependent children. There is also an earnings related supplement in cases where sickness benefit would have been payable but for payment of injury benefit. After 26 weeks a person who is still incapacitated may be able to claim sickness benefit, and invalidity benefit, as well as disablement benefit.

The injury must have arisen out of and in the course of employment. This covers most injuries at work. If the accident occurs at work it is assumed that it arose out of the employment unless there is evidence to the contrary. Whether one is considered to be at work when away from the place of employment depends on the circumstances. Travelling to and from work is not normally included, unless the transport is provided by the employer.

The accident should be reported to the employer at once - failure to do so may make it difficult later to establish what happened. The actual claim should be made to the local Social Security office within six days, if possible together with the doctor's statement. A person who has not previously claimed sickness or injury benefit can claim within 21 days. There are special arrangements for someone who cannot claim because he is in hospital. For details see Leaflet N1.5.

The industrial injuries scheme applies also to employees who suffer from one of a list of prescribed diseases. There are over 50 such diseases - they are listed in Leaflet N1.2. There are special provisions which apply to pneumoconiosis (including silicosis and asbestosis) and byssinoisis - see Leaflet N1.3 - and to occupational deafness - see Leaflet N1.207.

One of the special provisions in regard to pneumoconiosis, asbestosis, silicosis and byssinosis is that under legislation passed in 1979 lump sum compensation can be obtained from the Secretary of State for Employment if the workman's employer has gone out of business and cannot be sued - see the Pneumoconiosis, etc., (Workers Compensation) Act 1979.

Employees who suffer disablement because of an accident at work or an industrial disease resulting from work can claim *disablement benefit.* Payment starts after injury benefit has ceased but it can apply also to those who never receive injury benefit because they do not need to go off work. The amount of the benefit depends on the extent of the disablement. This is assessed by a medical board. Normally relatively minor disablement is dealt with by a lump sum and more serious conditions by a weekly pension.

There are a number of additional allowances:

● *Special hardship allowance* to compensate a person who cannot go back to his normal job or to similar work.

● *Constant attendance allowance* if the disability is 100 per cent. and as a result there is a need for constant assistance.

● *Exceptionally severe disablement allowance* payable to those who have an exceptionally bad condition where attendance is likely to be permanent.

● *Hospital treatment allowance* for those whose condition is being treated in hospital.

● *Unemployability supplement* for those likely to be unemployable permanently. (This benefit cannot be claimed in addition to special hardship allowance, unemployment, sickness or invalidity benefit or retirement or widow's pension).

On benefits for industrial injuries and diseases generally see articles by Mark Rowland in *LAG Bulletin*, 1980, pp. 35, 87, 161, 262.

Where an employee dies as a result of an accident at work or a prescribed industrial disease his widow or other dependants can claim a non-contributory *industrial death benefit*. This consists of a basic weekly sum plus in some cases an earnings related addition. See Leaflet N1.10.

10. *INJURIES CAUSED BY CRIME*

As has been seen, anyone injured by a violent criminal act may have the right to ask for compensation paid by the Criminal Injuries Compensation Board. Application is made to the Board at its address 10-12 Russell Square, London WC1B 5EN. A claim can also be made where the injuries occur whilst trying to prevent a crime or assisting the police. If the injuries result in death the claim can be made by dependants.

The level of compensation is assessed on the same basis as common law damages. The amount therefore depends on the degree of injury, the extent of any loss of earnings or out-of-pocket expenses and of pain and suffering.

The Board issues a leaflet, *Crimes of Violence - A Guide to the Compensation Scheme*. Claims are made on an application form CICB.2 obtainable from the Board.

11. *SOCIAL SECURITY FOR THE HANDICAPPED OR DISABLED*

There are various special forms of payments in respect of the handicapped and disabled:

Attendance allowance is payable where a person over the age of 2 is severely disabled, physically or mentally, and has to be looked after for over 6 months. There are two rates - one for day and night attendance, the other for day or night attendance. Information is available in Leaflet N1.205. Claims are made on the form in the leaflet.

Invalid care allowance is paid to men or single women of working age who cannot go to work because they have to look after a severely disabled relative who is getting attendance allowance. Information is provided in Leaflet N1.212

and claims are made on the form in the leaflet.

Mobility allowance is payable to people between five and pension age (65 men, 60 women) who are unable or almost unable to walk because of disablement. Information is given in Leaflet N1.211 and claims are made on the form in the leaflet.

Assistance with fares to work can be claimed by a severely disabled person who incurs extra expenses in getting to work because of his disability. The claim can be for a contribution to the cost of taxis or chauffeur driven hire car. Leaflet DPL.13 obtainable from a Jobcentre or employment office has more information. Claims can be made through the disablement officer at the local Jobcentre or employment office.

Rate relief can be asked for by anyone (including owner occupiers) whose premises have had to be altered because of disablement. Application forms should be obtainable from the local council.

Free milk for handicapped children is available for children who do not go to school because of their disability. Form FW.20 from a local social security office is used for such claims.

Miscellaneous other cash benefits and services exist to help the handicapped and disabled. These include free or reduced cost bus and train fares, day nurseries, holidays, home helps, meals on wheels, laundry services, provision of television sets or telephones etc. See Leaflet HB.1.

Help for handicapped people should be available from the local social security office.

12. *RETIREMENT*

When a person reaches retirement age (men 65, women 60) he or she is entitled to a state pension if they have retired from regular work. (One does not have to give up work completely, provided earnings do not exceed the amount allowed under the earnings rule). A person receives the pension if over 70 (men) or 65 (women) whether they are still working or not. Delaying one's pension until 70 (or 65 for women) increases the amounts payable.

Claims for a pension should be made some three to four months before one reaches pension age. Failure to make a timely application can result in delays and loss of money. Claims have to be made to the local DHSS office. For details see Leaflet NP.32, NP.32A (for the widowed or divorced), or NP.32B (for married women).

Those who reach pension age after April 1970 and have paid standard rate contributions since April 1978 will also get an additional earnings related pension.

Those who are in a contracted out occupational pension scheme run by their employer will get their additional pension from that scheme. The right to this pension is protected even on change of job.

Those who paid contributions between 1961 and 1975 may also get graduated retirement benefit.

Married women may be entitled to a pension on their own national insurance contributions or on their husband's contributions or both. (See leaflet NP.32B).

If the pension does not give enough to live on, application should be made for a supplementary pension. Leaflet SB. 1 explains the details and has a claim form.

Special services for the elderly include home helps, meals on wheels, aids to mobility, day centres and special transport schemes. The local council's social services department should have all details of what is available in the district. Senior citizens can apply for a British Rail card which substantially reduces the cost of train travel. Details are available from British Rail.

13. *WIDOWS*

There are four main types of social security payments for widows:

Widow's allowance is paid in the first six months of widowhood on the husband's national insurance contributions. The allowance is paid at a flat rate with addition based on average earnings of the deceased husband and a further increase for dependent children. Leaflet NP.35 explains the details and claims should be made on form BW.1. The allowance is not available to widows over 60 or to those whose husbands were retirement pensioners.

Widowed mother's allowance is payable to a widow of any age who has at least one qualifying child under 19 or who is expecting a child by her late husband. A qualifying child is, broadly, one for whom the widow or her husband were entitled to child benefit. The allowance is based on the husband's national insurance contributions. (See Leaflet NP.36 for details). It is payable from the time that widow's allowance ceases and has a basic rate plus a sum for each qualifying child. If the husband died after April 1979 the widow can also get any additional earnings-related pension he had earned. Claims are made on form BW.1.

Widow's pension is paid to widows aged 40 or over when widowed who have no dependent children or who are 40 or over when widowed mother's allowance ends. It is based on the husband's national insurance contributions. The amount varies depending on the age of the widow. If the husband died after April 1970 she can also get any additional earnings related pension he had earned. Leaflet NP.36 gives the details and claims are made on form BW.1.

Death grant is a lump sum paid to the next of kin, executor or other person paying the funeral expenses of the deceased. The grant depends on national insurance contributions - for details of who is covered see Leaflet N1.49. (The leaflet *What To Do After A Death*, D.49 is also useful as a general guide).
Widows need advice on many aspects of their situation but one in particular is on national insurance contributions and benefits. The chief problem requiring attention is whether to

pay reduced contributions or to opt instead for full liability.
Leaflet N1.51 gives some valuable guidance on the issue.

14. *ADJUDICATION AND APPEALS IN SOCIAL*
SECURITY CASES

In national insurance cases the initial decision is made by an
insurance officer appointed by, but independent of, the
Secretary of State for Social Services. The claimant can
appeal against the insurance officer's decision to a local
tribunal and a further appeal from the tribunal's decision lies
to a Social Security Commissioner (formerly known as
National Insurance Commissioner) at the instance of the
insurance officer, the claimant or his trade union "or any
other association [of which he is a member] which exists to
promote the interests and welfare of its members" - including, presumably, a claimants' union.

The Social Security Act 1980 provided that appeals from
unanimous decision of a local tribunal to a Social Security
Commissioner would only lie with leave either of the chairman of the tribunal or with the leave of the Commissioner. It
also stated that appeals from the decision of a Commissioner
would lie on a point of law to the Court of Appeal - but again
only with the leave of the Commissioner or of the Court of
Appeal.

The same system of adjudication and appeals applies to
claims for *child benefits* and, with the exceptions mentioned
below, *industrial injuries benefits*.

Claims for *attendance allowance* are referred to the
Attendance Allowance Board for a decision as to whether
attendance is needed to the extent specified in the Act. The
Board's decision on this question is binding on the insurance
officer and the local tribunal; but the Board can be asked by
the claimant to review its decision, and an appeal lies to the
Social Security Commissioner on a point of law arising on
such a review.

The *industrial injuries* scheme provides for "disablement
questions" - whether a particular accident has resulted in a

loss of faculty, the degree of disablement, and the period for which it is to be assessed - to be decided by a medical board, with a right of appeal to a medical tribunal. Similarly, on a claim for injury benefit, the claimant can appeal to a medical board against the insurance officer's decision that he is not suffering from a prescribed disease, with a further right of appeal to a medical tribunal. An appeal against a medical tribunal's decision, on a point of law, lies to the Social Security Commissioner.

Certain questions are reserved for decision by the Secretary of State for Social Services. These include the classification of insured persons as employed, self-employed or non-employed; whether an employment is insurable for the purposes of the industrial injuries scheme; the amount of reckonable earnings for the purpose of calculating earnings-related supplements, whether contribution conditions for any benefit are satisfied; whether a disablement pension is to be increased by constant attendance allowance and, if so, for what period and what amount. There is a right of appeal on a question of law to a High Court judge.

Decisions on claims for *supplementary benefit* and *family income supplement* were formerly made by the Supplementary Benefits Commission. But as has already been seen the Commission was abolished in 1980 and decisions on individual cases are made by supplementary benefit officers. This in practice continues the previous system under which cases were determined by an official at the local Social Security office on behalf of the Commission. More difficult questions may be referred to the regional office or head-quarters of the Department of Health and Social Security.

An appeal from a decision of the supplementary benefits officer can be made to a local Supplementary Benefit Appeal Tribunal which, unlike National Insurance Tribunals, sits in private. The appellant has a right to be present and may be accompanied by not more than two persons, either or both of whom may represent him, or he may be represented in his absence. The tribunal's decision can now be further challenged on a point of law by appeal to a Social Security Commissioner and thence with leave to the Court of Appeal.

Time limits are laid down for claims, but failure to make

the claim within the prescribed period need not be fatal providing that "good cause" can be shown. The tribunals have, however, developed somewhat technical and narrow definitions as to what constitutes good cause. (See *LAG Bulletin*, October 1974, p. 240; and Martin Partington, *Claim in Time*, (1978)).

8 The Consumer and Defective Goods or Services

1. INFORMAL PRESSURES

On buying something defective the first step is to complain to the person who sold them. In many instances, reputable concerns will remedy the defect either by taking the goods back, replacing them or by repairing them.

If this does not prove successful, informal pressure can sometimes be brought to bear through a trade association or through a local consumer advisory group, consumer advice centre, or Citizen's Advice Bureau.

2. RETURNING THE GOODS

Once a contract of sale or hire purchase has been concluded, the seller cannot normally be legally required to take the goods back *even if they are defective*. There are only four main exceptions.

One is where the goods were brought on the doorstep under a hire-purchase or credit-sale agreement for less than £2,000. In such cases, the customer has four days in which to change his mind - the "cooling off" period. But this only applies if the contract was signed away from the dealer's or finance company's premises. It does not apply, therefore, if the arrangements was agreed on the doorstep but actually signed down at the office.

The second exception is where the goods are so defective as to be fundamentally useless for the purpose for which they were intended. A car or washing machine or other consumer item that simply does not work at all could be returned and the money paid demanded back. In such a case the purchaser need not take any replacement or credit note. Providing he cancels the agreement promptly he is entitled to have his money back in cash. If the money has already been paid, it can be demanded back, though if the shop refuses to pay, the only remedy may be to sue. The buyer is in a much stronger position if he has not yet paid for the goods or is paying by instalments. He can then refuse to pay or stop the instalments, as the case may be. If the shop then sues him he can resist the action by a defence that the goods were fundamentally defective. But if the item is not totally useless, but merely somewhat defective, the law does not require that the seller take it back, but merely that he give back part of the money paid, by way of compensation.

The third main exception is where the buyer has been induced to buy by a false statement of fact - a misrepresentation within the meaning of the Misrepresentation Act 1967. So, if a second-hand car dealer says that the car has only done 35,000 miles when in fact it had done 55,000, the buyer can revoke the contract and get his money back if he can show that this misrepresentation was instrumental in getting him to buy. It is not necessary to show that the seller knew the statement was false, but the seller has a valid defence if it was reasonable for him to believe the statement was true. The remedy of revoking the contract on the grounds of misrepresentation only applies, however, if it is sought quickly. If an unreasonably long time has elapsed the only remedy will be an action for damages.

A fourth exception is where the seller has specifically said that money will be returned if the customer is not satisfied. This means that the customer can insist on getting his money back.

Of course, if no contract has yet been concluded the goods can always be returned. This may happen, for instance, with unsolicited goods sent through the post. The recipient of such goods has two choices. Either he can notify the sender that he does not wish to have the goods and give the address from which they can be collected. If they are not collected within thirty days from the date he posts his letter, the goods become his in law. Alternatively, he can simply keep the goods safely for six months without notifying the sender. If at the end of six months they have not been collected, they become the recipient's property and he need not pay for them. Any attempt to get him to pay for goods he has not ordered or agreed to buy is a criminal offence.

Goods sent on approval (as a result of a newspaper advertisement, for instance), can always be returned and any deposit claimed back. But obviously the recipient is liable for any damage to the goods which occurs whulst they are in his possession. If a signature is required on first receipt of the goods it is always wise to add the words "accepted unexamined" to protect against the danger that they may be damaged when first opened.

3. *REPAIRS UNDER GUARANTEE*

Goods are frequently sold under guarantee. This is normally an arrangement between the purchaser and the manufacturer. Sometimes it only applies if the guarantee registration card is returned within a stated period. Invariably it only operates for a limited period, commonly six months from the date of purchase. If, for any reason, the guarantee does not apply to the particular situation, it does not mean that there is no possibility of a claim against the seller or even the manufacturer. The buyer's legal rights against the seller are unaffected by whether or not there is a guarantee by the manufacturer. Moreover, the manufacturer cannot exclude his liability for injury or damage caused to others than the buyer by negligence in the manufacture of the goods. The manufacturer can say that the buyer took the goods subject to the terms of the guarantee, but if others (such as members of the buyer's family or his friends) suffer, they cannot be affected by the terms of a guarantee to which they were not a party. (See "Suing the Manufacturer" p. 136 below.)

4. *COMPENSATION FROM THE SELLER OF DEFECTIVE GOODS*

Ordinarily, the only remedy provided by law for the purchaser of defective goods is to sue the seller for damages for the difference in value between what was paid for and what was received. This means that the consumer himself must take the initiative and bring an action (for guidance as to how an action can be brought see p. 170 below). Alternatively, if he has not yet paid for the goods or is paying for them by instalments, he can withhold payment and wait to be sued or, alternatively, can continue paying after deducting the price of making the necessary repairs. He is legally liable for the full purchase price but he is entitled to bring a counterclaim for the cost of repairs plus any consequential costs or expenses. In practice, this is often a better course of action for the seller may decide that it is not worthwhile to bring in the courts and if he does, less trouble and expense may be involved in defending than in taking the proceedings.

Since the Criminal Justice Act 1972 a consumer has the further right to get damages by way of compensation through a criminal prosecution. This has the advantage that it will be cheaper and simpler to get the weights and measures inspect-orate to prosecute in the magistrates' courts and to ask for compensation there than to bring an action in the civil courts. The chief situation in which this right is important to con-sumers is where there has been a false description of goods in breach of the Trade Descriptions Act. Most criminal proceed-ings under this Act so far have been in regard to purchases of cars as a result of false mileage or false descriptions of the conditions of the engine.

The law previously placed limits on the right of the seller to exclude liability by an exclusion clause in the contract. Both in an ordinary agreement of sale whether for cash or credit and in hire-purchase contracts the law implied a basic condition that the goods are of merchantable quality, which means that they are of reasonable quality for the purpose for which they are intended having regard to their price, descrip-tion and nature. This condition could not be excluded in a sale to an ordinary consumer unless the defects were specif-ically drawn to the buyer's attention or, where the buyer inspected the goods, in regard to defects that he noticed or ought to have noticed in his inspection . But the 1977 Unfair Contract Terms Act went even further by banning "exclusion clauses" by which traders purport to limit or exclude their liability in the fine print of a contract. Any such clause put into a contract by a trader acting in the course of his business is void. The act applies to attempts to exclude liability for death or injury in any contract or attempts to exclude liability in consumer contracts for failure to supply goods that meet the description applied to them or terms relating to the quality or fitness of the goods supplied. Exclusion clauses designed to avoid liability arising out of negligence are only enforce-able if "reasonable" having regard to all the circumstances. The Act provides a significant form of new protection to the consumer.

5. *DAMAGES FROM THE MANUFACTURER*

The normal remedies for defective goods are available to the buyer against the seller but, in certain circumstances, an action for damages may lie against the manufacturer. This is where the manufacturer has been guilty of negligence and someone (whether the buyer or someone else), has been injured as a result. An action will lie against the manufacturer, providing the injury was a reasonably foreseeable consequence of the negligence. So, if the man of the house buys an electric iron and his wife receives an electric shock because the iron was improperly wired, she would be able to sue for damages. Such an action would not preclude legal proceedings against the retailer as well. Indeed, where two persons appear to be liable it is often wise to proceed against both; this avoids the danger that if, for any reason, one action fails, the other will not be lost through failure to start it in time.

6. *PROSECUTING THE RETAILER*

In certain circumstances the seller may have committed a criminal offence for which he could be prosecuted. He may, for instance, have been guilty of selling food that is unfit for human consumption, or that is short in weight. It is also an offence to give a false trade description or a false indication of price, whether or not with intent to mislead. In all these cases complaint should be made to the local weights and measures inspector.

A new form of consumer protection introduced in the Fair Trading Act 1973 is against unfair trade practices. Once the Secretary of State has made an order prohibiting a particular commercial practice as unfair, in that it is misleading, confusing or inequitable, any breach of such an order is a criminal offence. The enforcement of such orders is again a matter for the inspectors of weights and measures.

In addition, the Act established a new official, the Director-General of Fair Trading to supervise the whole consumer field. Any evidence of sharp practice by retailers should be brought to the attention of his office - Field House, Breams Buildings, London EC4, Tel: 01-242 2858. It is the duty of his office to examine any practices which adversely affect the interests of consumers. In particular, he will be on the look-out for such practices as misleading advertisements or undue pressure to accept burdensome or illegal or ineffective conditions in contracts.

9   Abortion

An abortion is legal if permitted under the Abortion Act 1967. This says that two doctors must agree that *one* of four alternative conditions apply:

(i)   that continuation of the pregnancy would create a risk to the mother's life;

(ii)   that continuation of the pregnancy would endanger the mother's physical or mental health more than if the pregnancy were terminated;

(iii)   that continuation of the pregnancy would endanger the physical or mental health of any other children of the family more than if the pregnancy were terminated;

(iv)   that there is a substantial risk that the child would be born with a severe physical or mental abnormality.

A woman desiring an abortion should first consult her own doctor or, failing this, some other general practitioner. The second opinion is frequently that of a consultant. Some consultants will see patients without the prior introduction of a general practitioner.

Abortions conducted under the National Health Service cost nothing. Those done privately usually cost over £100 and sometimes much more. But abortions conducted for a charge through one of the abortion advisory services cost less. These services have grown partly to help women whose local doctors are unsympathetic to the idea of abortion.

Among the main advisory services are: Pregnancy Advisory Service, 40 Margaret Street, London W1N 7FB; Marie Stopes Memorial Centre, 198 Whitfield Street, London W1P 6BE; Pregnancy Advisory Service, 1st Floor, Guildhall Building, Navigation Street, Birmingham B2 4BT; and Southern Pregnancy Advisory Service, 138 Dyke Road, Brighton, Sussex BN1 5PA.

10 Sex and Race Discrimination

1. *SEX DISCRIMINATION*

The Equal Pay Act 1970 and the Sex Discrimination Act 1975 came into force at the end of 1975.

The 1970 Act implies an "equality" clause in contracts of employment. The effect of this clause is to give a woman remedies for breach of contract if she is treated less favourably than a man for "like work" or for work "rated as equivalent" to that done by men.

The 1975 Act bans sex discrimination in various fields. In employment it relates to recruitment, promotion opportunities, training, or other benefits or services. The Act applies to companies, partnerships, trade unions, qualifying bodies, vocational training bodies and employment agencies.

The 1975 Act also bans sex discrimination and marriage discrimination in education, housing, and the provisions of goods and services.

There are, of course, exceptions. Thus, in the employment field it is permitted to discriminate on the grounds of sex in provisions for death or retirement, or in employment in private homes or where the number of employees is not more than five, or where sex is a genuine occupational qualification (*e.g.* for acting a role in dramatic performances, or in single sex prisons or hospitals). In the educational field there are exceptions for single sex schools. The provisions relating to housing do not apply in small dwellings where the person offering the accommodation intends to continue living on the premises. Genuine clubs not conducted for profit can remain single sex. Where the main object of a voluntary body is to benefit members of one sex it is not unlawful to carry out that object.

The agency responsible for the overseeing of the entire area is the Equal Opportunities Commission, Overseas House, Quay Street, Manchester, M3 3HN, Tel: 061-833-9244. The

Commission issues leaflets giving guidance on the Acts and their enforcement.

Proceedings to challenge instances of alleged discriminations must be taken in different ways depending on the field concerned. Employment matters are handled primarily through industrial tribunals, other fields are dealt with by county courts. Notice of any court proceedings must be given to the Commission and a copy of such a notice must be filed with the court. In cases of alleged discriminations by public educational bodies, the Secretary of State for Education must be notified and proceedings cannot be started until he has indicated that he does not need further time or two months have elapsed (whichever is the shorter).

A complaint must be brought within six months of the act alleged to constitute unlawful discrimination, but there is power to waive the time limit if it is just and equitable to do so.

Complainants can ask the respondent to fill out a questionnaire requesting further information. (Details can be found in the Sex Discrimination (Questions and Replies) Order 1975 (S.I. 1975 No. 2048).) If these questions are put before proceedings are started they must be served on the respondent within six months of the act in question or three months in employment cases. Such a questionnaire can be a powerful weapon in the hands of the complainant.

The Commission can investigate alleged discriminatory practices and can issue "non-discrimination notices" ordering discrimination to cease. Non-compliance can result in enforcement procedures in the county court.

Damages can be claimed for actual loss suffered and also for wounded feelings.

For a practical guide to problems of sex discrimination see *LAG Bulletin*, 1977, pp. 83, 106, 133, 159.

2. *RACIAL DISCRIMINATION*

The Race Relations Act 1976 makes it unlawful to discriminate directly or indirectly on the grounds of race, colour, nationality or national or ethnic origin in the provision of housing, employment, education, qualifying tests for any profession or trade, trade union membership, or the provision of goods, services, or facilities to the public or any section of the public.

The Act does not apply to employment in the private home, nor where the discrimination can be justified as being a genuine occupational qualification. The Act does not apply to residential accommodation in small premises where the landlord or a near relative is living on the premises and shares certain accommodation with the lodgers or tenants. (Small premises are defined as those where the landlord shares with one or two households, or where he shares with up to six other persons).

Clubs and other associations of more than 25 members may not discriminate in regard to admission to membership or the treatment of members or associates.

The Act also bans discriminatory advertisements.

Enforcement is partly in the hands of complainants and partly of the Commission for Racial Equality (whose offices are at 10/12 Allington Street, London SW1. Tel: 01-828 7022). The Commission has powers to institute its own inquiries and to issue non-discrimination notices to persons found to have carried on a pattern of discriminatory conduct over a period of time.

A complainant can bring proceedings on his own behalf. If the matter relates to employment, such an action must be brought in the industrial tribunal; otherwise proceedings are brought in selected county courts. In the employment field the services of conciliation officers are available to attempt to arrive at an amicable solution to the problem.

The county court can grant an injunction, issue a declaration, or order damages including compensation for injured feelings. The industrial tribunal has the power to award damages (similar to those available in the county court) or to issue a declaration or to order that the offending party take action to avoid or reduce discriminatory conduct.

As in the case of sex discrimination, the Act provides for a preliminary questionnaire to be administered by the complainant to the other side as a means of disclosing basic facts.

Complainants who are in doubt as to how to proceed should consult with the Commission which has power to advise and assist complainants in the preparation or conduct of proceedings. (See generally G. Bindman, *LAG Bulletin*, September 1977, p. 213; October 1977, p. 236).

11 Wills

1. *IS IT WORTHWHILE TO MAKE A WILL?*

Most clients with whom social workers have professional contact have little or no property and rarely consider making a will. But even with the smallest estate the question may not be irrelevant. A man living with someone not his wife who wishes to leave her part of his property must make a will. A woman who has been abandoned by her husband to bring up their children may, for instance, be anxious to make a will to see that he does not inherit anything after her death - even though the total value of her property may be extremely small.

If there is no will or if the will is invalid, property is distributed according to fixed rules laid down by statute. Under these, if there are children, the surviving spouse takes the first £40,000 absolutely. Since many estates, even in these days of inflated house values, are under £40,000 this rule covers the ordinary situation. If there is more in the estate and there are children, the surviving spouse takes all personal effects, the first £40,000 and a life interest in half the remainder, while the children (including any illegitimate children) take an equal share in the other half of the excess over £40,000. A life interest means that the money can be invested and the income spent but the capital cannot normally be touched.

If there are no children, the surviving spouse takes the personal effects, the first £85,000 and half of any remainder. The remaining half is shared between the deceased's parents, if still alive; if they are dead, the brothers and sisters share it. If there are no parents, children, brothers or sisters, the widow or widower takes all.

The main point of making a will, therefore, is to provide for a cohabitee, to avoid one's property going to the surviving spouse or in order to make special provision for relatives or friends who would otherwise receive nothing, or less than the appropriate amount. If, for instance, a widower has adult children, three of whom are in a secure financial position but one of whom is mentally retarded or physically disabled, the father may wish to leave his small estate entirely to the one child who really needs the money.

2. *MAKING A WILL*

A will can be made by anyone over the age of 18 who is of sound mind. Relatives who believe themselves to be unfairly treated can challenge it on the ground of the mental incapacity of the testator, but in the absence of evidence to the contrary, it is always assumed that the maker of the will was of sound mind.

A will must be in writing. There is no requirement, however, that it be drawn up in formal language, nor that it be drafted by a solicitor nor that it be witnessed by any formal or official procedure. It is, however, vital that the terms of the will be drafted clearly. A will form can be bought from stationers, but the danger of these is that their standard terms often need adaptation to suit the needs of the particular situation. Solicitors do not in fact charge very much for drafting wills - £8 to £20 for a simple case and the work can be done under the new (green form) legal advice and assistance scheme (see p. 15 above).

If the will is home-made there are certain basic rules that must be observed:

1. The will should open with a statement that it is the testator's last will and testament. ("This is the last will of John Smith of Holly Lodge, Okehampton Street, Liverpool 15 and was made on June 23, 1980."). If any previous will has been made, a statement should be added revoking any such will. (" I hereby revoke all former wills and codicils.")

2. The will should nominate one or more persons to act as executors to handle the distribution of the estate. Their prior agreement to act is desirable. ("I hereby appoint Wilfred Brown of 14 Acacia Drive, Liverpool 13 and Arthur Gold of 93 Lower Road, Birmingham 9 to be executors and trustees of my will.")

3. The will should dispose of the property. ("I bequeath £100 and my gold watch to my eldest son Richard and the same sum and my books to my younger son, Ernest. I leave £50 to the Hambledon Cricket Club to be used for club teas

in my memory while the money lasts. I leave the residue of my estate to my wife, Margaret.")

4. The will *must* be properly signed and witnessed. It must be signed by the testator in the presence of at least two adults, sane witnesses who are not beneficiaries and who must themselves sign in his presence. There should also be a clause specifically stating that this procedure was complied with. ("Signed by the testator in our presence and then by us as witnesses in his presence John Smith, Testator; Mary Woods of 14 The Close, Highbury Road, Liverpool 11, housewife; Elizabeth Jane Holland of 19 Wexford Road, Liverpool 12, housewife.")

If a beneficiary or the husband or wife of the beneficiary signs as witness, the gift to them under the will fails. Witnesses do not need to see the contents of the will. They are merely acknowledging the testator's signature, not what he has written. But they must see him actually signing.

The signatures should be on the last page of the will at the end of the text. Anything written after the signatures is invalid.

Once made, a will can only be validly altered by an addition or codicil which is signed and witnessed in the same way as the will itself. But there is no need for the witnesses to be the same.

3. *CHALLENGING A WILL*

If the will has been made properly and there is no evidence that the testator was of unsound mind or was brought under the improper influence of someone such as a solicitor, it will normally be virtually impossible to upset the will.

But it may be possible to get the will varied. A family member who was a dependant can ask the High Court for an order that some part of the estate be devoted to their support.

This might happen, for instance, where a testator leaves his whole estate to a cat's home. The wife can make an application for some support either by way of lump sum or regular payments or both. This remedy used to be confined to dependent family members, but under the Inheritance (Provision for Family and Dependants) Act 1975, it now covers a spouse, a former spouse not remarried, any child whether or not dependent, anyone treated as a child of the family (*e.g.* a step-child) or anyone who was being wholly or partly maintained by the deceased at the time of death - including someone with whom he was cohabiting.

The application must be made within six months of the date probate was granted or letters of administration were taken out. If the net estate is under £5,000 the county court has jurisdiction; if it is more both the Chancery and the Family Divisions have jurisdiction. A solicitor should be consulted as to the way in which the application should be presented.

12 Employment

1. *OBTAINING A JOB — THE CONTRACT OF EMPLOYMENT*

Under the Employment Protection (Consolidation) Act 1978, an employer must give his employee a written statement within thirteen weeks of starting work of certain terms of the arrangement between them. The matters that must be covered are the following:

1. The names of the parties — the employer and the employee.
2. The date when the job began.
3. Whether employment with a previous employer counts as continuous employment with the present employer, and if so, the date on which the previous job began.
4. Details of wage and piece rates for the job.
5. An indication whether wages are weekly, daily, hourly or what.
6. The hours of work.
7. Details of holidays, holiday pay, sick pay and (if there is one) of the occupational pension scheme.
8. Provisions regarding notice.
9. The title of the job.
10. Any disciplinary rules which affect the worker.
11. Explanation of how any grievance machinery works.

The written statement is *evidence* of the contract - not the contract itself. But if a worker signs a statement that the document sets out all the terms of the agreement, he will not be able to allege later that in fact it did not. Also, the Court of Appeal has held that a simple receipt signed by the worker saying that he has had the written statement makes it into a contract.

There is no penalty for failure to provide the written statement and many employers, especially smaller ones, are in default.

The law implies into every contract of employment certain terms whether or not they are expressed. Thus, the employee must exercise skill and care in his work, must be honest and must not do anything which prevents him from doing his work, nor must he disclose confidential information to anyone outside the company. The employer must provide safe premises and methods of work. (On implied terms see *LAG Bulletin*, March 1979, p. 62; on express terms see *LAG Bulletin*, November 1979, p. 264.)

A worker is entitled to be paid in actual money. The employer can only pay by cheque, giro or other means of credit transfer if the worker has requested this in writing. The employer is not allowed to make any deductions save those approved by statute and for those owed to someone else, where the worker has asked for this to be done.

2. *DISCIPLINE DURING WORK*

Sanctions imposed by an employer for misconduct (actual or imagined) are only legal if they are permitted by the contract and the law. The worker could sue for damages if he were made the victim of illegal sanctions or penalties.

Fines or deductions from pay will normally not be lawful unless they are genuinely based on the actual or estimated loss to the employer caused by the employee's act.

Suspension with pay would normally be lawful.

3. *DISMISSAL*

The old common law rules about dismissal have in recent years been drastically altered by statutes designed to improve protection for workers.

Notice

The Employment Protection (Consolidation) Act 1978

specifies *minimum* periods of notice which apply unless the employee's conduct is such as to justify instant dismissal. If the employee has been with the employer for under 4 weeks, or if the total contemplated period of employment was under 12 weeks, there is no notice requirement. But otherwise the employee is entitled to at least one week's notice for each year of service up to a maximum of 12 weeks for 12 years' service. Anyone who has been employed for 26 weeks at the date of dismissal is entitled to have written grounds for the dismissal.

A worker is not bound to accept wages in lieu of notice. If he does not agree to do so and the employer does not want him around, the employer must pay him his weekly wages. If he stays and works through the period of notice he is entitled to his proper wages.

Unfair Dismissal

Where an employee has worked for his employer for 52 weeks or more, his dismissal is presumed to be "unfair" entitling him to compensation, unless it can be justified on one of five grounds:

(i)   The worker's ability and qualifications for his work;
(ii)   The employee's conduct at work;
(iii)   Redundancy (see p. 150 below);
(iv)   Continued employment would contravene a statutory requirement;
(v)   Some other substantial reason justifying dismissal.

If the dismissal cannot be brought within one of these five categories it is automatically treated as unfair and entitles the worker to compensation or re-instatement. If it is brought within one of the five grounds, it is still for the tribunal to decide whether the employer acted reasonably in treating the ground as requiring dismissal. In deciding this the tribunal may have regard to the Code of Practice issued by the Department of Employment.

If the employee is dismissed for a single isolated act of misconduct, his dismissal will often be held unfair. It will also normally be unfair if he has not had adequate notice of the charges against him and opportunity to answer them.

A person may be dismissed for striking providing he is not

victimised or unfairly discriminated against. Employees who work less than 16 hours a week are not covered by the unfair dismissal law - unless they have been employed for over five years in work requiring more than eight hours a week. The Employment Act 1980 also excluded small firms starting in business after the Act came into force during the first two years of trading.

Claims go to the industrial tribunals - consisting of a legally qualified chairman and two others.

Claims must be brought within three months of the dismissal, unless the tribunal is prepared to extend it on the ground that it was not practicable to make the application within the three-month period. The dismissal for this purpose occurs on the date on which the period of notice expires. The claim is brought only when it is actually received by the tribunal. It has been decided, however, that ignorance of the law can in some circumstances be a valid excuse for not bringing the claim in time.

The normal remedy is compensation. *Compensation* is assessed on two bases - the basic award and the compensatory award. The basic award (maximum £3,300) is designed in most cases to include an element equal to a full redundancy payment. No award can be made for a redundant worker who unreasonably refuses, or who has taken suitable, alternative employment or where he unreasonably refused an offer of reinstatement or where the tribunal considers it is just and equitable given the complainant's conduct either before or after dismissal. The award is otherwise calculated like that for redundancy - see below. If redundancy payment is paid this must be taken into account. The basic award cannot be for more than 26 weeks' pay. If however dismissal is on the ground of race, sex or trade union activity, punitive damages of up to 52 weeks' pay can be ordered in addition to the basic award.

Compensatory payment is additional - and is based on actual loss up to a maximum of £6,250 after deduction for the employee's own fault. (The £6,250 maximum is over and above the basic award). Claims are based on such things as loss of wages, actual or prospective, or fringe benefits (such as use of a car, free meals, pension rights) expenses (moving house, travelling to look for other work); loss of seniority; and future losses that are likely to follow. If the employee has contributed to his own dismissal, the claim will be reduced.

Also the employee is under a duty to "mitigate his loss," which means that he must take all reasonable steps to get another equivalent job.

One of the purposes of the recent legislation on unfair dismissals (notably the Employment Protection (Consolidation) Act 1978) is to encourage industrial tribunals to secure, wherever possible, that employees are reinstated. The tribunal must ask whether the employee wishes to go back to the firm and if so, it may make an order for reinstatement or re-engagement. ("Reinstatement" is to be treated in all respects as if the dismissal had not taken place; "re-engagement" is to be re-employed on comparable work.) But a survey by the Department of Employment showed that in 1977 of the 35,389 who made a claim of unfair dismissal more than half got nothing, 27 per cent. of the claims were withdrawn and 25 per cent. were dismissed by the tribunal. Of those who got compensation the amount typically was under £400. Only 2 per cent. were re-instated.

If the worker is reinstated, or re-engaged, but the employer does not fully comply with the order, the industrial tribunal can order "additional compensation" in such amount as seems fair. If the order for reinstatement or re-engagement is not complied with at all, the tribunal must make a basic award and must consider whether a compensatory award should be made.

Damages for Wrongful Dismissal

"Unfair" dismissal is now the chief basis for claims arising out of loss of employment (other than redundancy). But there will still be some cases where the employee will prefer to sue instead or in addition for wrongful dismissal under the old common law. This would be so especially in the higher reaches of management where employment contracts are for a fixed period of years and a claim under the unfair dismissal procedure may not provide adequate compensation. The damages would be for the wages or salary he would have earned less the tax he would have paid.

Redundancy

The second main reason for claiming compensation is where

the ground of dismissal is redundancy.

Redundancy means that the job in question has ceased to exist. Redundancy payment is made even if the employee finds alternative employment at once. It is tax free and is paid in one lump sum.

Those who qualify must be between 18 and 65 and must have worked for the employer for at least 16 hours per week for over two years.

Claims must be made within six months of the date of dismissal. It is vital that an employee who is given notice on the ground of redundancy, should work during the full period of notice or that, if he leaves during the period of notice, it should be with the full consent of his employer. Otherwise he loses his right to claim redundancy pay. If he is offered another job with the same firm he should accept only on a trial basis. There is a four-week trial period. If he finds it unsuitable within that period, he can then still claim he has been made redundant. But he must refuse to do the new job and be sacked. If he resigns of his own accord in disgust, he will lose his right to claim.

The compensation is based on the length of service with the employer. For each complete year of service from the age of 41 to 65 (60 for a woman), he is entitled to one and a half weeks' pay; for each completed year of service from age 21 to 41, he is entitled to one week's pay; for each completed year of service from age 18 to 21, he is entitled to half a week's pay. The maximum payment is £3,300 and £120 is the highest weekly pay that can be considered. The maximum period that can be counted is 20 years. Payments are reduced for those declared redundant in the last year before pension age.

Claims are usually made with the help of the union, but if the union officials do not assist, the employee should consult with the local office of the Department of Employment. Disputes between the workman and the firm are determined by an industrial tribunal.

A worker can get compensation for redundancy *and* unfair or wrongful dismissal. For a practical guide to unfair dismissal and redundancy cases see *LAG Bulletin*, 1977, pp. 11, 39, 60, 81, 108, 162, 182, 234.

Racial or Sex Discrimination

If dismissal is thought to have been on the grounds of race, colour, ethnic or national origin there may be the basis of a complaint to the Commission for Racial Equality (see p. 141 above). As has been seen, this could lead to compensation.

In sex discrimination cases complaints go, in the first instance, to conciliation officers who attempt to arrive at an amicable settlement.

13 Handling a Criminal Case

A social worker's involvement with a client's criminal case is likely to start after the charge has already been laid. The client is arrested, charged and released on bail from the police station or he is detained in custody and members of his family want to know what can be done to assist him.

1. *IS DETENTION FOR QUESTIONING LEGAL?*

If he is held by the police but no charges have been preferred, a suspect is, in the time-honoured newspaper euphemism "helping the police with their inquiries." In law this means that unless he is there voluntarily he is under arrest - whether or not the police admit the fact. English law does not recognise any position between being under arrest on reasonable suspicion of a stated offence and not being under arrest (in which case one is legally free to go). The police do quite commonly hold suspects for questioning for some time before deciding whether to charge them. Under existing law there is no specific time limit for such arrest but a person beng held without charges against his will is entitled to ask a High Court judge for a writ of habeas corpus to secure his release. If he is being held incommunicado, someone else can make such an application on his behalf. A lawyer's help will be essential. Since 1977 the police have been under a duty to notify someone reasonably named by the suspect of the fact of his arrest and of his whereabouts.

A child under 14 is supposed, where possible, to be interviewed by the police in the presence of a parent or guardian or, failing this, someone other than a police officer. A school child is not supposed to be interviewed or even arrested on school premises.

2. *ACCESS TO A LAWYER IN THE POLICE STATION*

The Judges' Rules provide that a person in police custody should be permitted to contact a solicitor or friend, provided this does not unreasonably hamper the process of police investigation. The police tend to interpret this to mean, "You may consult a solicitor when we have finished questioning you." There is little that can be done about this - apart from complaints by lawyers for the defence in court.

If the police permit a suspect to contact a solicitor, and the solicitor is willing to come to the police station, the attendance and advice comes within the legal advice and assistance scheme (see p. 15 above). Also, a member of the family can, of course, consult a solicitor on behalf of the suspect and can instruct him to act in the case.

3. *IS IT WORTH APPLYING FOR LEGAL AID?*

If the case is to be heard at a Crown Court, it will always be worth applying for legal aid and such an application will almost always be successful unless the defendant has considerable means (see pp. 18, 20 above).

If the case is to be heard before magistrates, whether it is worth applying for legal aid will depend on the particular circumstances.

Situations in which the defendant should be advised to apply include:

● where the likely range of penalties seems quite serious;

● where he intends to plead not guilty to anything other than a trivial charge;

● where a conviction would result in loss of a job or other benefit;

● where the defence will require any considerable effort of preparing the case, tracing witnesses, conducting scientific tests, etc.;

● where the defendant seems unlikely to be able to do himself justice if he has to speak for himself.

Sometimes it may be sensible to have a word with a lawyer (even over the telephone) to discuss whether, in the actual cicumstances of the case, legal representation is desirable. (For how to apply for legal aid, see p. 22 above.)

If the defendant is not represented by a lawyer, he is entitled to come to court with a friend or other assistant (who might be a social worker), to help him, for instance, by making suggestions or taking notes (see p. 11 above).

4. *TO PLEAD GUILTY OR NOT GUILTY?*

Defendants quite frequently plead guilty to charges to which they claim to be innocent. They do so in order to get the matter over with more quickly, with less publicity and with less cost. They may feel "The court is going to take the word of the police rather than mine, so what's the use of fighting it." Also, they may have discovered that the courts tend to deal more leniently with those who plead guilty. All of these assessments may be true - but no one should ever be *advised* to plead guilty to something he has not done. Certainly no lay adviser should ever get into the position of giving such advice. A person who is wrestling with this dilemma should always be counselled to talk it over with a solicitor. With the solicitor's help it may be possible to make a successful fight of it.

A similar problem occurs when the defendant pleads guilty to a more serious offence than he has in fact committed. It is not uncommon for the police to charge a person with a variety of offences, some more serious than others. The defendant who has a lawyer may be able to make a deal with the prosecution, to plead guilty on condition that the more serious charges are dropped. This plea bargaining is more difficult for a defendant to engage in effectively without a lawyer and this is another reason why anyone faced with charges that are at all serious should be advised to consult a solicitor.

5. *GETTING BAIL*

Bail may be obtained from the police station after the defendant has first been charged. After he has first appeared in court, however, the question of bail lies not with the police, but only with the magistrates. The question arises whenever a criminal case is adjourned, whether before trial, during trial or after the trial pending sentence.

Under the Bail Act 1976, there is now a statutory pre-

sumption that bail will be granted. This means that on a
remand the defendant is entitled to bail unless good reason
can be shown for him not to get bail. The presumption
applies, also, to remands after conviction, pending sentence.
Many defendants are unaware of their right to apply for bail.
Many are also quite ignorant about what it involves. The
most common misconception is that the amount of bail has
to be produced in the form of cash. In fact, no money has to
be handed over at all except where there is thought to be a
risk that he will go abroad and not come back in which case
he can be asked for security. Release on bail used to be made
subject to a recognisance entered into by the defendant and a
further commitment from sureties. So, the magistrate would
grant bail to the defendant in his own recognisance of, say,
£25 and two sureties of £50 each. This meant that the
defendant and his two sureties promised to pay the named
sums in the event that the defendant failed to turn up.
Whether they were in fact required to pay that amount
depended on the discretion of the court, but they had to
appear to be able and willing to pay. The 1976 Bail Act
abolished the defendant's own recognisance. Instead, it
introduced a new criminal offence of absconding whilst on
bail. Also, if bail is granted subject to conditions, there is a
new power in the police to arrest the defendant and to bring
him back to the court if he is not obeying those conditions.

Where the police do not object to bail, it is usually granted.
Where the police do object it is usually refused. Grounds for
refusal are usually variations on one or more of a number of
themes - that the defendant will skip (because of his bad
record, the seriousness of the offence, his lack of stable
community roots or the fact that he has previously done so);
that he will commit further offences (because of his bad
record); that he will interfere with witnesses; or that further
inquiries need to be made.

A juvenile (under 17) who is remanded in custody, must
be committed to the care of the local authority where he
lives or where the offence occurred unless the court certifies
that he is too unruly to be committed to care. If such a certificate of unruliness is issued, the juvenile can be remanded to
a remand centre, if no place is available in a prison, or, if the
remand is to be no more than 24 hours, in a police station.
No remand to a remand centre or prison can be validly made,
wihout a certificate of unruliness.

If bail is refused once, there is nothing to prevent a later application to the same court and this can sometimes be successful. However, the Divisional Court ruled in May 1980 that on a second or subsequent remand hearing the court should only have regard to new factors. It should not reconsider facts previously taken into account. On the other hand, there is, as will be seen, a right of appeal.

If the accused is represented by a lawyer, the points that can be made in favour of an application for bail will usually emerge. When he is unrepresented they often do not. The most important evidence to support an application of bail is that the accused is not likely to vanish pending the trial. The magistrates should therefore be informed of any favourable facts, for instance that the defendant has lived in the same premises or held the same job for six months, one year, or more; that he lives with wife and children, or that he sees family members regularly; that he has no prior record, or only a minor record; that he has previously been released on bail; that there are special circumstances which make bail desirable, such as pregnancy of a wife, ill-health of a relative, or the fact that the defendant is responsible for looking after minor children.

If anyone can be found who is willing to become a surety he should be asked to come to the hearing. The police should be notified as soon as possible so that they can consider whether the person put forward is acceptable as a surety. Becoming a surety is obviously a risk and many people are understandably reluctant unless they know the defendant well enough to be confident that they will not be let down. If the surety cannot come to the hearing the police in the area where he works or lives are usually willing to vet him and to inform the police dealing with the defendant's case whether he is acceptable.

Apart from sureties, it is often helpful to have character evidence from one or two respectable persons in the community - an employer, clergyman or suchlike. They too must be asked to come to the actual hearing since the court will only take account of anything they have to say if they are physically there.

There is a right of appeal to a judge in chambers if bail is refused. If the defendant is willing to pay the fees (at least £35 and probably more), he can instruct his solicitor to handle the appeal. (Legal aid is not available for bail applications or refusal of bail, save that under the Bail Act 1976 legal aid can be granted where a person is to be remanded a second time in custody.) If he does not have the money, an appeal can be made through the Official Solicitor. The forms should be available in all prisons but this form of appeal very rarely succeeds since the accused person has no opportunity to put his case to the judge in person. He speaks only through the form he fills out and few appellants have much idea as to how to complete the form in such a way as to persuade the judge to reverse the refusal of bail.

The fact that bail has once been refused does not mean, however, that it cannot be successfully applied for at a later stage. This is particularly so if the refusal was based on a prosecution claim that further inquiries had to be made. After one or two remands of eight days each (no pre-trial remand in custody can be for longer), the magistrates may be persuaded that the police have now had ample time to make their inquiries and that the original reason for refusing bail is no longer applicable.

6. *PREPARING THE CASE*

If the defendant who intends to plead not guilty is represented by a solicitor, the preparation of the case will be handled by the lawyers. If not, the accused person may need some guidance as to how he should go about the business of getting his tackle in order.

The main advice is that he should consider what evidence he needs to support his story. If, for instance, his defence is an alibi, he will have to get the person or persons he was with at the critical time to agree to testify. If they refuse, he can get a witness summons or subpoena to compel attendance at court. To get such a subpoena, application must be made to the court at which the case is to be tried. The cost, which is very low, includes an appropriate amount to cover the witnesses' travel expenses to and from the court, plus an amount for compensation for loss of time. These amounts are calculated according to a scale depending on the distance to be travelled and the witness' occupation.

A witness must normally attend in court to give his evidence and it is the accused person's responsibility to see that his witnesses get to the right place on the right day.

If the evidence in question is purely formal and not contested by the police the witness' time can be saved by avoiding the need for him to come to court. This is under a special procedure laid down in the Criminal Justice Act 1967. The witness' statement must be taken down in writing and must be signed by him. At the foot of each page of the statement the witness must write and sign: "The contents of this page are true to the best of my knowledge and belief and I know that I am liable to be prosecuted if they are false or known to be untrue." One copy of the statement must then be sent to the police and another copy to the court clerk. The police are allowed to require that the witness be called for cross-examination, but if they do not make such a request the evidence can be read at the trial.

Even if the witness is coming to court, it is advisable for the defendant who is conducting his own case to have a full written version of the witness' proposed evidence. The witness cannot read the statement, but the defendant, after calling him to give evidence, can use the written statement as the basis for his questioning.

7. *WHICH COURT TRIES THE CASE?*

Criminal cases can be dealt with either in a Crown Court or in a magistrates' court. The most serious can be tried only in the Crown Court; the most minor can only be taken in the magistrates' courts. But there are many offences which can be taken in either court. The defendant is entitled to ask for trial by jury in all cases which are triable at either the higher or lower level - Criminal Law Act 1977. There is little point to this if he intends to plead guilty but on a not guilty plea there are certain advantages.

A juvenile normally has to be tried in the juvenile court even for indictable offences. The only exceptions are where he is charged jointly with an adult and it is felt necessary, in the interests of justice, that they be tried together, or if the offence is one for which an adult could get 14 years or more imprisonment. A juvenile therefore, has no right to trial by jury, save in the most serious cases.

One advantage of being tried in the Crown Court is that the prosecution has to produce enough evidence, in advance, to establish a prima facie case, whereas the defence can keep its case secret until the actual trial. The only part of the defence case that has to be disclosed in advance of the trial is an alibi. Secondly, the facts are found by a jury of 12 ordinary citizens instead of the magistrates. (It used to be thought that the acquittal rate before juries was higher than before magistrates but the available statistics suggest that this may not be so.)

The third main advantage is that it is easier to get legal aid for a trial at the higher level.

On the other hand, Crown Court cases mean additional delay - which in some parts of the country, especially London, may be considerable. Trial before the magistrates normally can be had more quickly.

The powers of sentencing available to magistrates are less than those that can be used by the Crown Court. But this is not a reason to prefer trial at the lower level, for if at the end of the case the magistrates decide their powers of sentencing are inadequate, they can send the defendant for sentence to the higher court.

The choice between trial at the Crown Court or at the magistrates' court is one that should be made, if possible, on the basis of legal advice. If the trial is at the Crown Court, the accused will normally be legally represented.

8. *TRIAL BEFORE MAGISTRATES*

If the defendant is legally represented, the actual handling of the case will be undertaken by the lawyer and there will be nothing for the social worker to do. But if the defendant is not represented, the social worker concerned with the case may be able to assist the defendant, at least by explaining the procedure.

Pleading not guilty

If the defendant pleads not guilty, the case opens with the prosecution evidence. At the end of each witness' evidence the defendant will be given an opportunity to ask the witness questions (to cross-examine). It is obviously not feasible to train the ordinary defendant to master the art of cross-examination, but he should be told two basic points. One is that he should challenge anything in the witnesses' evidence with which he disagrees. If he fails to do this he may not be permitted to testify to a different effect when it comes to his turn to give evidence. (Magistrates vary in the extent to which they insist on strict compliance with the rules of evidence and procedure.) So, if the witness says that he saw the defendant striking the complainant a blow about the head and the defence case is that the blow was actually struck by someone else, the accused must put it to the witness that he was mistaken. The witness will probably deny that he was mistaken, but this does not matter. The crucial thing is that the way is now open for the defendant, when he gives his own version of the incident, to say that it was someone else who was responsible for the injury.

The second point, is that cross-examination is not the moment for the accused to give his own evidence. He should limit himself at this stage simply to asking questions designed to undermine or weaken the prosecution case.

In order to assist the process of asking questions it is advisable that the defendant note down, while they are giving evidence, the issues on which he wishes to challenge the witnesses.

When all the prosecution witnesses have given their evidence, the defence are entitled to submit that there is no case to answer. Normally, however, the submission is rejected and the court says it wishes to hear the defence before making up its mind.

In the case of trials of children between 10 and 14, the prosecution must prove not only that the accused committed the offences but that he knew his act was wrong. If this is not proved, the child is entitled to be acquitted because the prosecution will not have rebutted the presumption that a child under 14 does not know right from wrong.

The defendant will then himself give evidence. He should prepare this in advance in writing - though he will not be allowed to read it out. But by writing it out he will get his thoughts into the best order for presentation to the court. When he has completed his own evidence, the prosecution may cross-examine. The accused will then call and examine his own witnesses.

When asking questions of one's witnesses, leading questions which suggest the answer, are not permitted. So, for instance, the witness cannot be asked "It was raining wasn't it?" or "I didn't hit him did I?" or "I was driving at 30 mph wasn't I?" Instead, he must ask "What was the weather?" or "Did you see me hit him?" or "At what speed would you say I was driving?"

Witnesses can usually only give evidence about what they saw or heard themselves - not of what was seen or heard by someone else and reported to them. This is the "hearsay" rule.

At the end of the evidence for the defence, the prosecution and the defence (in that order) have the right to sum up by summarising the evidence and the questions for the court. It is legitimate to remind the court that for the case to be proved it must be satisfied beyond a reasonable doubt.

The decision of the court will usually be given either immediately or after a short adjournment. If the accused is acquitted he is entitled to ask that his costs be paid out of public funds, though this will not necessarily be allowed. If he is conducting his own defence such costs will normally be extremely small.

If he is convicted, the magistrates will turn to the passing of sentence, though often they will first remand the case for reports.

Pleading guilty

On a guilty plea, the prosecution gives a brief outline of the facts and then turns to the question of sentence.

Sentence

Before sentencing the defendant the magistrates will be prepared to listen to anything that can be said in mitigation. Most defendants are quite incapable of presenting an effective plea in mitigation for themselves. It is therefore most desirable that someone be available to assist at this stage. A social worker has no right of audience as such but, if present, the court may be prepared to listen to information from such a source or from other persons such as employers, former or present teachers or anyone else respectable who can say something relevant. Obviously, from the defence point of view, there is no point in bringing a character witness unless he can speak well of the defendant. It is always desirable for the defendant to have character witnesses to speak for him; moreover, there is no reason to limit such evidence to one witness if two or even more good ones can be found.

In juvenile courts the defendant or his parent or guardian can be asked to leave the court whilst reports are read if this is thought to be in the best interests of the juvenile. But the court ought to tell the juvenile or the parent the substance of any such report and give an opportunity for further evidence to be given on the child's behalf in regard to matters raised.

Since 1973 the criminal courts have had power to order compensation to be paid by the defendant to the victim. In the magistrares court the maximum amount is £1,000. (See *LAG Bulletin*, July 1978, p. 162). There is also a power to order restitution of stolen goods to the person from whom they were taken. (See *LAG Bulletin*, December 1978, p. 291.)

14 Actions in the County Court

1. *BEING SUED*

Well over one and a half million cases are brought annually in the county court. Since large numbers of claims are settled prior to the issue of any legal proceedings, the total number of actual claims being pursued each year must run into many millions.

It is usually preferable for a claim to be settled out of court than to be fought to a finish - though this is not true if a settlement results in one side paying money to the other which is not legally due. The case that goes to court is the rare one that is resisted.

(a) *Pressures for Settlement*

The system provides various pressures and devices that promote out of court solutions to claims. One is the device known as "without prejudice" negotiations. The words "without prejudice" on the top of any letter exchanged on the subject of the claim means that anything in the letter is privileged so far as concerns any subsequent court case. Another device is payment into court. Where the defendant, in personal injury cases wants to settle he can pay say, £1,000 into court. This constitutes an offer of settlement of the case. If the sum is accepted, that is the end of the matter. If it is not, and at the trial the claimant recovers more than £1,000 the loser has to pay the costs of the entire action. But if he recovers less than £1,000 then, in spite of having won, he has to bear all costs of the case from the date of payment in. In other words, payment is a lever to settlement through the pressure of costs. The defendant pays in less than he thinks the claim is worth but enough to tempt the claimant to accept. The claimant must calculate the odds of getting more than the sum paid in against the possible penalty in costs if he gets less.

Assuming, however, that settlement does not take place, legal proceedings may be instituted.

(b) *Receiving a County Court Summons*

A summons will be an ordinary summons or a default summons. (It says in the top left-hand corner which it is.) An ordinary summons demands the presence of the defendant at court on a stated date; a default summons says that judgment will be given without further notice unless the amount of the claim is paid within 14 days. Default summonses are very much more common than ordinary summonses.

The summons will normally be accompanied by two other documents. One is the particulars of claim which sets out the details of the claim. The other (Form 18A) is the form of Admission, Defence or Counterclaim. This requires that the defendant consider whether or not he wishes to resist the claim.

(c) *Whether to Resist the Claim*

There is little advantage, other than a gain in time, in fighting a claim that is well-founded. Also, resistance in a hopeless cause may simply cost the defendant more money. The summons itself will have marked on it the courts costs payable by the defendant. If the whole amount claimed is paid into court, the defendant will not normally be liable for any court costs or legal costs for the other side over and above what is stated on the summons. If payment is only made after a judgment there would be additional court costs and additional costs for lawyers' fees. So, for example, where the claim is for an amount between £100 and £1,000 and the costs are "fixed," the solicitor can claim £6 where judgment is given by default, £12 where the defendant has admitted the claim and the plaintiff has accepted his proposals as to mode of payment, £15 where the court has to decide questions of date of payment or rate of instalments and £20 where judgment is given after a contested hearing. If the costs are "assessed" by the court the amount allowed can be between £23 and £35 where the claim is under £200, between £25 and £50 for claims between £200 and £500 and £38 for claims between £500 and £1,000.

However, if the claim is for less than £500 it would normally be dealt with by arbitration (p. 176 below), in which case the loser can only be ordered to pay the costs stated on the summons, the costs of enforcement and any costs he is deemed to have incurred through his own unreasonable conduct.

The claim may be admitted, but the defendant may not have the means to pay it off. In such circumstances he should make an offer on Form 18A of payment by instalments. The offer has to be accompanied by details of pay, deductions, outgoings, payments under other court orders and other regular commitments. It is important not to make an offer of an unrealistically high amount; usually even low offers are accepted. If the claimant does not accept the offer there will normally be a hearing to decide if the amount offered is fair.

If the claim is partially but not wholly admitted, it is advisable to pay something into court, in order to reduce liability for costs. This again can be signified on the Admission section of Form 18A. Payment has to be by cash or postal or money order, cheques are not accepted.

But if the claim is not admitted or if the defendant has his own counterclaim, the defendant should fill out the Defence or the Counterclaim section of Form 18A. If he contests the claim altogether, he will enter a defence - for instance, if he denies having ever taken the loan or incurred the debt or having caused the accident. If he admits the claim, but says he wishes to set it off against a claim of his own, he will fill in the Counterclaim section - for instance, where he admits buying the goods but says they are defective.

Legal aid is not often available for small cases in the county court but if the case is for any substantial amount it may be worth considering an application (see pp. 17-22 above).

(d) *Judgment in Default of Defence*

If the defendant enters no defence or does not attend at the court hearing, judgment may be given against him for the full amount of the claim plus costs. The order of the court demanding payment will then be sent to the defendant. If payment is not made, the court will order enforcement procedure - including, in the last resort, seizure of the defendant's property and effects and their sale to satisfy the judgment. The normal method of enforcing a judgment today, however, is by an order whereby the employer deducts a stated amount from the weekly wage.

If the defendant receives a copy of a court judgment without ever having had the original summons, he is entitled to ask the court to cancel the judgment. He can also do this if he gets the summons so shortly before the date of the hearing as not to permit him time to do anything about it, or if he only sees the summons after judgment - for instance, because he was away abroad.

A person in this position should go immediately to the court to apply to have the judgment cancelled.

(e) *Defending the Claim*

If the defendant decides to resist the claim, he is entitled to consider whether the court in which it is being dealt with is the most convenient from his point of view. If not, he can ask that the case be transferred to one that is closer to his home - because of the cost or inconvenience that would otherwise arise for him. The application is by letter to the registrar of the court with a statement of the reasons.

The second step is to fill out the Defence or Counterclaim sections on Form 18A. If further space is needed the account can be continued on separate pages. The form of the Defence or Counterclaim should follow in general outline the plaintiff's particulars of claim. Facts which are not contested should be admitted; facts which are contested, should be denied. ("The facts stated in Paragraph 9 and 11 are denied" or "It is admitted that the plaintiff paid the defendant the sum of £100 but it is denied that this was by way of loan.")

The defence should be returned to the court within 14 days. If the case involves less than £500 it will normally be referred to arbitration (see below).

(f) *Arbitration*

Arbitration was introduced in October 1973. If the claim is for less than £500 (formerly £200) the registrar will automatically order arbitration - but either side can apply for the case to be heard at a normal trial if in all the circumstances this seems more appropriate and the registrar can be persuaded.

The object of arbitration is to provide a simpler and cheaper form of decision which is also less formal and is private. The arbitrator will usually be the judge or the registrar but someone else agreed on by the parties can be approved by the court. An outside arbitrator would, however, normally require a fee whereas the judge or the registrar would not be paid anything by the parties.

One advantage of arbitration is that whereas court proceedings are normally in public, arbitration is in private. Another is that the arbitrator can accept evidence (such as written evidence or "hearsay") that would not be admissible in an ordinary court. The actual hearing will be less formal - the arbitrator will not wear a wig or gown. The decision is fully enforceable but there is not so full a right of appeal.

An ordinary person proposing to bring or resist a claim would probably be well advised to accept arbitration, unless he wants a public hearing.

(g) *Preparing for the Hearing*

After the defence and any counterclaim have been sent into the court, a date will be fixed for a pre-trial review. This is a preliminary hearing at which both sides attend so that the court can consider how the issues can be simplified and what directions can be given to ensure that the case is heard with maximum efficiency. The review is taken in private. If the defendant does not attend, judgment can be given there and then for the plaintiff. If the defendant does attend, the registrar will decide whether to order trial or arbitration and will fix a date for the hearing.

Each side will then get into shape for the hearing. Witnesses should be approached for statements and must be asked whether they are prepared to come to court. A written statement from the witness will normally not be sufficient (save perhaps in an arbitration). If the witness is reluctant to come to court, he can be compelled to do so by a witness summons which is obtained from the court, on payment of 60p for the issue and service of the summons. An appropriate amount will also have to be paid for the witness' travel and loss of time. Whoever wins the case will normally have the costs of his witnesses paid ultimately by the loser.

If the claim involves special expertise in, say, plumbing, electrical work, cars, etc., it is often desirable to bring an expert to support one's case — though he will normally require a fee for doing so. This is one of the expenses that the loser normally has to pay at the end of the case. The loser can be required to pay up to £10 for pre-trial preliminary work and up to £20 for attendance at court by an expert.

If the expert has prepared a report before the case, it may be desirable to show it to the other side to ask whether they are prepared to accept it without requiring the expert to come to court. If the other side does agree, the written report can be used as evidence without the expert being present to be cross-examined. If the other side does not agree, the expert must attend.

Relevant documents such as letters, contracts, paid cheques to prove payment, invoices, etc, should be assembled and brought for the hearing. If the claim concerns an item of equipment, this can either be brought to the hearing or, if this is impossible, can be inspected by the court prior to the hearing. Arrangements for this can be made at the pre-trial review (see p. 168 above).

(h) *The Hearing*

It is always wise to get to the hearing well before the scheduled time to allow time to find one's bearings. The unrepresented litigant is permitted to bring a family member, friend, social worker or other person as aide and assistant. Such a person can advise, take notes, make suggestions and even, with the permission of the court, speak for the litigant.

The hearing begins with the plaintiff or claimant stating his case. This must be done from the witness-box. The story should be told as simply and clearly as possible. At the end the claimant's account he can be questioned (cross-examined) by the defendant (see p. 160 above). The claimant then calls his other witnesses who give their evidence from the witness-box and are questioned. At the end of the claimant's case the defendant and his witnesses give evidence and in their turn are cross-examined.

Finally, the judge gives judgment - usually without any adjournment. Whoever wins will be given his costs, which means that the loser must pay the reasonable expenses of the winner. Court fees will be paid in full unless the recovery was for less than the claim in which case the fees appropriate to that sum will be allowed. In regard to witnesses, one can recover a reasonable amount for their attendance at the court hearing and travel costs. One may also claim reasonable reimbursement for maps, plans, photographs, fares, telephone calls and other incidentals. As has been seen, on an arbitration the costs allowable to the winner are very restricted. After an ordinary hearing the winner can claim higher costs - the exact extent of which will depend on the amount involved. (Lower Scale for amounts under £200, Scale 2 for sums between £200 and £500, Scale 3 for £500 to £1,000 and Scale 4 for claims over £1,000.) They can be either fixed costs or costs assessed by the court. The higher the Scale, the higher the costs.

From 1976, a successful litigant in person has been able to claim for time spent on his own case other than in an arbitration where he recovers less than £500. The amount recoverable is limited to two-thirds of what would have been charged by a solicitor. If the litigant in person has not suffered financial loss by doing the work, he is limited to a maximum of £2 per hour. Details can be obtained from leaflets prepared by the Lord Chancellor's Department and issued to the courts.

As a general rule, no one should be encouraged to undertake litigation lightly. It is commonly a frustrating and exasperating experience even for the winner. Not only does it create anxieties, it also frequently costs a good deal of money, and if the case is contested, the outcome is often uncertain. On the other hand, anyone with a potential legal remedy for a wrong he has suffered should consider carefully whether the remedy should be abandoned simply because to pursue it may be troublesome. The game may be well worth the candle. This is especially true when one considers whether to take up a claim for damages for something reasonably precise such as a personal injury caused in an accident or an unpaid debt. Were there is doubt as to whether or not the case should be taken or defended, it may be worth seeking professional advice simply on this point. A lay adviser such as a social worker can play an invaluable intermediary role in counselling a client with actual or potential litigation in the county court and in helping to make the experience less traumatic.

2. *BRINGING AN ACTION*

The county courts are rarely used by ordinary citizens to bring actions. Most people seem to be either too nervous to use the machinery of the courts for their claims or too conscious of the cost. Very recently, however, three steps have been taken to make actions easier and less frightening to bring.

One is the introduction of the new arbitration procedure (see pp. 167-168 above). The second is the new rule that where a case is referred to arbitration, the loser cannot normally be required to pay any costs over and above the court costs fee and a nominal fee of £8 - £18 depending on the amount involved for solicitor's fees plus a further small sum in respect of enforcement procedures. In other words, a claimant who conducts his own case and loses should normally not have to face more than a small bill. In fact whether the litigant wins or loses, if the costs are too high, there is a little known right to apply to the Lord Chancellor under section 5 of the County Court Fees Order 1975. This says that "where it appears to the Lord Chancellor that the payment of any fee would owing to the exceptional circumstances of the particular case, involve hardship, he may reduce or remit the fee in that case." (For guidance as to the procedure to follow see *LAG Bulletin*, June 1980, p. 141.)

The third recent development has been the publication of a guide for the person wishing to take (or defend) proceedings without a lawyer. Put out by the Lord Chancellor's office and available from county courts, it is free of charge (*Small Claims in the County Court*). It should be consulted by anyone considering taking legal action without the help of a lawyer. In spite of recent cuts there are still many consumer advice centres to advise citizens in addition to Citizens' Advice Bureaux and also lawyers under the "green form" legal advice scheme, p. 15 above.

The kinds of situation in which action might be contemplated are if someone refuses to pay a debt, or to return money loaned, where goods bought turn out to be defective, where a builder, garage or other repairer has failed to do the work or has done it badly; or where injury has been suffered through someone else's negligence.

Before taking action it is normal to write making the claim and inviting the other side to acknowledge it. Only if there is no appropriate response are legal proceedings started.

Obviously, it is necessary to know the full name and address of the person against whom the proceedings are brought (the defendant). In the case of a company the full name and reigstered office ought to be on the notepaper. Failing this the address can be obtained from the Companies Registration Office, Crown Way, Maindy, Cardiff CF4 3UZ.

If the action is against a firm or partnership, it should be brought against the firm without naming the partners individually. The address is that where the firm does business or of the individual partners. The names and addresses of the partners should be available from the Registry of Business Names, Pembroke House, 40-56 City Road, London, EC1Y 2DN.

Action can be brought in the court in the area where the defendant lives or carries on business. Or it can be brought in the district where the action arose - where the accident took place, the debt was incurred, or the contract was concluded.

Commencing an action involves court fees for the issue of the summons depending on the value of the claim. In the High Court the issue of a writ from July 1980 costs £35 if the sum claimed is under £2,000 or £40 if the claim is for more. In the county court it is 10 per cent. of the amount claimed with a minimum of £2.50. If the claim is for a sum between £201 and £300 the fee is £21; for each further rise of £100 the fee goes up by another pound save that for sums over £500 it stays at £24. Where the proceedings are not for money the maximum fee is £24. In addition a small fee is payable for service of the summons by the bailiff.

If the claim is for a specific stated sum of money, it will be made by a default summons otherwise it will be by ordinary summons.

The court clerks will usually be very helpful in guiding the litigant in person through the procedure. There is also now a free pamphlet available from county courts on enforcing judgments - *Enforcing Money Judgments in the County Court.*

3. *TIME-LIMITS FOR SUING*

All actions in the civil courts must be brought within a time-limit. These time-limits vary from one kind of case to another:

1. Actions for personal injury - three years from the accident or, if later, from the date when the claimant had know-ledge of the possibility of making the claim. Knowledge for this purpose means knowing that the injury was significant and that it was attributable in whole or part

to an act or omission by a known person. A person is deemed to have knowledge if it would have been reasonable for him to have acquired it, but not where the relevant facts could only be discovered by experts and he had taken all reasonable steps to take such advice. Where injury results in death an action can be brought within three years of the date of death or within three years of the personal representatives acquiring knowledge whichever is the later. Such an action is in respect of any claim by the deceased himself. Claims by dependants for loss of dependency can likewise be made within three years of the date of death or of the claimant having knowledge of the claim, whichever is the later.

2. Actions arising out of contract - six years from the breach of contract.
3. Debt - six years from the date the debt was incurred or when the debtor last admitted liability.
4. Civil wrong - libel, slander, trespass, wrongful withholding of property - six years from the date of the wrong.
5. Recovery of land or eviction of squatters - 12 years.
6. Recovery of rent - six years from the date of last unpaid rent.

If the person entitled to take legal action is under 18 and in the custody of a parent the time-limit runs from the date when he becomes 18. If the person concerned is of unsound mind and he recovers, the time-limits run from the date of his recovery except that the six year limit is then reduced to three years.

There is normally no time-limit in criminal cases. Nor is there any time-limit for an action by a beneficiary under a trust against a trustee for fraud or return of the assets of the trust.